Essential
Florida

by
CAROLE CHESTER

PASSPORT BOOKS
a division of *NTC Publishing Group*
Lincolnwood, Illinois USA

Published by Passport Books, a division of NTC Publishing Group, 4255 West Touhy Avenue, Lincolnwood (Chicago), Illinois 60646–1975 U.S.A.

The contents of this publication are believed correct at the time of printing. Nevertheless, the publishers cannot accept responsibility for errors or omissions, nor for changes in details given. We are always grateful to readers who let us know of any errors or omissions they come across, and future printings will be updated accordingly.

Published by Passport Books in conjunction with The Automobile Association of Great Britain.

Written by Carole Chester
"Peace and Quiet" section by Paul Sterry

Library of Congress Catalog
Card Number 93–85629
ISBN 0–8442–8909–4

10 9 8 7 6 5 4 3 2 1

PRINTED IN TRENTO, ITALY

Front cover picture: Disney World

The Automobile Association would like to thank the following photographers and libraries for their assistance in the compilation of this book.

J ALLAN CASH PHOTOLIBRARY 14 Art deco, 16 Vizcaya Mansion, 21 Key Biscayne, 22 Seaquarium, 30/1 Key Largo, 39 Edison Museum, 41 Sanibel Island, 45 Boardwalk & Baseball Theme Park, 59 Madeira Beach, 62/3 Sponges at Tarpon Springs, 72 Kapok Tree Restaurant, 76 Canaveral wildlife reserve, 84 Remains of sugar cane mill, 86/7 Jupiter Island, 89 Flagler Museum, 89 Door ornament, 92/3 St Augustine, 95 St Augustine Church, 112 HMS Bounty.

INTERNATIONAL PHOTOBANK 4 Disney World, 9 Miami Beach, 18 Bird of Paradise Flower, 35 Key West Church, 47 Disney World Mickey, 48 Disney World Magic Kingdom, 52 Sea World, 55 St Pete Beach, 56/7 Clearwater Beach, 61 St Petersburg, 64 Hotel Don Cesar, 69 Busch Gardens, The Python, 80 Anhinga Trail, 101 Fairchild Tropical Gardens, 116 Macaw.

NATURE PHOTOGRAPHERS LTD 104 Heron, 107 Great white heron, 109 Barred owl, Screw Pines (Paul Sterry).

SPECTRUM COLOUR LIBRARY 6 EPCOT Center, 7 Indian statue, 25 Parrot Jungle, 33 Hemingway House, 36 Fishing, 51 Gatorland Zoo, 53 Wet 'n' Wild, 70/1 Busch Gardens, 79 Snakebird, 82 Yachts, 94 Castillo de San Marcos, 100 Kennedy Space Center, 102/3 Alligator, 110 Oranges, 120 Rent a Car, 125 Windsurfing, Florida Keys.

ZEFA PICTURE LIBRARY UK LTD cover Disney World, 12 Miami, 27 Bayside Market, 29 Florida Keys, 81 Fort Lauderdale, 96/7 Sarasota, 98/9 Tallahassee.

CONTENTS

This book employs a simple rating system to help choose which places to visit:

◆◆◆ do not miss

◆◆ see if you can

◆ worth seeing if you have time

*Part of the Florida
magic: a ride
through the Magic
Kingdom at Disney
World*

INTRODUCTION

Florida has many facets: brash Miami Beach,
Cuban/Spanish Miami (the city proper), rich
Palm Beach, laid back Keys, soft West Coast,
and fun Orlando.

For tourists there are three great attractions:
the warm, sometimes sultry weather, the
theme parks and the low prices. It has a
plethora of family-oriented amusement and
entertainment complexes – Disney World
being perhaps the best known. Florida also
boasts the lowest car rental rates of anywhere
in the US – a factor that has helped produce a
wide variety and range of vacation packages
including fly/drive combinations.

Florida, though a southern state, has always
stood apart from the rest of the "deep south."
Here you can find a resort city which for
decades has featured top line performers in
its hotel supper clubs, and been patronized
by the wealthy jet set – all without the benefit
of casinos. Here there are beach-fringed
islands, loved by artists and writers,
fishermen and boating enthusiasts. And there

is also a wilderness which remained unexplored until the mid-19th century. Florida's main cities – Miami, Tampa and Orlando among them are well-known destinations, but the state has more still to offer.

In the historic northeast there are many state parks, several wildlife preserves and a national forest. There are rivers, countless lakes and a beach made famous by racing cars.

Racing, too, is a focal point of the central east coast, an area which also gave birth to the Kennedy Space Center.

The southeast is Florida's "Gold Coast," America's Riviera where a string of resort communities and marinas have blossomed; yet the 200-mile (320km) stretch of shoreline embraces two national parks and many state parks besides.

In the heartland of the state there is variety and adventure. This is fruit country, lake country, cattle country, horse country and fun country.

The west coast's sunbelt resorts are called the Pinellas and the region encompasses no less than 12 state recreational areas and a state forest. Finally, the northwest offers the Florida Panhandle, a narrow strip of sand and salt marshes where magnolias and mossy oaks grow.

Florida is a springboard to the Caribbean by air or luxury cruise liner, but within the state wheels are the biggest boon. There are accommodations to suit everyone, from expensive hotels, where to blink costs a dollar, to short term rental apartments and villas by beach or golf course, to casual guest houses.

This is the sunshine state, whose outdoor life has been developed for the vacationer's delight. Huge resorts with several golf courses; racetracks for horses, greyhounds and cars; houseboats, yachts and canoes, abound. Florida is a place where you have ample opportunity to see the sights, take up sports – or just relax.

If the pace is hurried at all, it is at Disney World and the adjacent EPCOT, both still growing, and offering so many alternatives that even a week here is not long enough.

The new Disney-MGM studios are the latest attraction and, while there, guests can watch movie production as it happens. The Studio Tour takes visitors through backlot streets, into sound stages where they can see the action from second floor soundproofed walkways and alongside post-production crafts, wardrobe and animation departments.

But Florida is not only beaches and theme parks – it has huge areas of unspoiled countryside where wildlife thrives; the Everglades is the most famous of these, but there are many others. So, if you want to get back to nature, or just have a yen to see an alligator, then Florida is the place for you. Juan Ponce de Leon, Puerto Rico's Spanish Governor, came to Florida in 1513 in search of the legendary Fountain of Youth. He didn't find it back in the 16th century, but perhaps if he were one of today's travelers he might have deemed his quest a complete success.

Spaceship Earth, at Disney World's EPCOT, takes visitors on a journey in time

BACKGROUND

Look at a map of Florida and
one of the first things you may
notice is the number of Native
American place names. Even
Miami is a name thought to be
derived from the Native
American words *maiha*
(meaning "very large") and
mih ("it is so") which led the
Spanish to mark their 17th-
century maps with *Aymai* or
Mayami.

At the time of Spanish
exploration there were around
10,000 Native Americans in
Florida, divided into four
tribes: the Timucuan and the
Apalachees who lived in the
central and northern territories,
and the more aggressive
Calusa and Mayimi in the south.
But Florida is best known for
the Seminoles (a name which
means "runaways"), originally
Creek Indians from Georgia,
who broke from their tribe and
took over this area.

Their ranks were swelled by
runaway slaves and, by the 18th
century, they had formed a
strong federation that occupied
some of the best land in the
interior. They caused little
trouble to British settlers, having
been offered land grants by
British financiers, but when
Florida was ceded back to Spain
after the Revolutionary War,
there were many clashes. Once
settlers decided they wanted
the land for themselves, violent
outrages became worse,
especially as attempts were
made to move the tribes people
west of the Mississippi. Before
long, incidents of outrage and
revenge became a series, and

*The Great Spirit, a reminder of native
American history in modern Miami*

that series a war; several wars,
in fact.

The Seminole Wars lasted for
seven years and cost a lot in
lives and money. The Native
American chiefs fought well,
but their only "reward" came
in later years when places
were given their names:
Osceola, for example, is today
a national forest. Those Native
Americans who were not
captured, killed or sent west,
fled deeper into the interior, to
what is now called the
Everglades. Their descendants
even now live in Florida, in one
of two recognized local tribes.
Florida was in the past a slave-
owning state, boasting cotton
and sugar plantations like its
southern neighbors, and by

BACKGROUND

1860 cotton was the basis of the state's economy. When Florida and its neighbors seceded from the Union it became the main food supplier for the confederate army. But there is little of the Old South mentality here today. What is most noticeable is resort development, for which the weather and the railway may be thanked. Two far-sighted developers, Flagler and Plant, made the first steps in the 1880s, paving the way for what was to become a year-round vacation state. Henry Flagler, for instance, built the pioneer hotel in Palm Beach – the Royal Poinciana, soon patronized by wealthy eastern seaboard society – convinced of the site's tourist potential. He proved to be right, for Palm Beach continues to be an oasis of luxury on Florida's east coast. While Flagler was busy on this coast, Henry Plant realized the potential in the western portion of the state and built the Tampa Bay Hotel in Tampa. But it wasn't until 1897 that Miami was able to open a plush hotel, the million dollar Royal Palm, at a time when Miami Beach was just a mosquito-infested swampy island between the ocean and Biscayne Bay.

It wasn't, however, until after World War I that real estate became big business in this part of the country. As with all such "finds," reports of profits and quick fortunes soon attracted the speculators. Between 1920 and 1930, Florida's population quadrupled, seeing faster growth than in any other state. Overnight, cheap land was expensive, former paupers became millionaires. The Depression ended all that, but Florida did recover in the 1930s, when paper mills were introduced and refrigeration plants allowed the best local product – fruit and vegetables – to be more widely marketed.

Farming turned cooperative and the citrus industry was regulated by law. Building resumed, *et voilà* – Florida was a star vacation destination. Florida's image as an international vacation playground is far more recent, and for this we can thank developers such as Disney, as well as preservationists who have kicked life back into faded and neglected areas like the Art Deco district of Miami Beach and Tampa's Ybor City district. We can thank entrepreneurial airlines for introducing Tampa as an alternative gateway, showing us parts of the state that up until a few years ago were a local secret. In addition, Florida's role as the world's busiest cruise gateway is increasing as new ships are added to fleets, bringing with them extra visitors to coastal resorts. Nowadays, one doesn't have to traipse to the Caribbean to discover a sand-fringed offshore island where the sun is warm and the water blue. The "Sunshine State" is by no means perfect – it even rains there sometimes – but it has proved it's a great place for good times.

MIAMI

Miami is a city of palm trees, warm sand and blue seas; yet it's also a cosmopolitan city full of banks and sky-high complexes. Here you can enjoy waterfront restaurants, marinas, pastel-colored hotels, and a boardwalk; and discover shopping malls, museums, an arts center – and traffic jams. This is both a vacation and business destination, with subtropical foliage and an international clientele. Miami is Florida's most sophisticated and busiest gateway.

Modest beginnings

But "Miami" means many things. It means downtown, it means "The Beach," it means the neighborhoods like Coral Gables and the island of Key Biscayne. To understand what is where, it is necessary to understand Miami's

Miami Beach – 10 miles of white sands along the Atlantic

development. It was a determined woman by the name of Julia Tuttle who sent Henry Flagler frost-free orange blossoms from Biscayne Bay when the Big Freeze of 1894 had destroyed most of the rest of Florida's citrus and vegetable crops. She was trying to prove her point: bring the railway south beyond Palm Beach and see – the weather is fine. She proved it, and in 1896, the railway link was completed and began to bring in materials and people. Miami became a city. By 1899, the old troops' parade ground was suddenly a golf course; electricity and the telephone arrived; and dredging allowed the harbor here to accommodate large ships. Miami Beach, on the other hand, was horticulturist John

MIAMI

Collins' dream. He tried to grow fruit here, and dredged the canal from Indian Creek to Biscayne Bay as a transport route. Having failed to achieve this goal he turned his hand to creating a residential community. In 1913 the first proper link, a 2-mile (3km) wooden bridge (Collins), joined the two growing communities. Now there was no looking back. Despite setbacks from hurricanes, the land boom raced ahead. In the 1920s, southern Florida was where everyone wanted to be. Poet George Merrick planned Coral Gable; Hialeah racetrack opened; hotels were constructed; a new air service inaugurated. Even so, it wasn't until the 1940s that more causeways were built across Biscayne Bay, including Rickenbacker to Key Biscayne. Much has happened since then to strengthen and maintain

Miami's position as a boom city and resort as well as a major convention destination. Transport systems have been improved and in the last few years vast investments have been made to inject glamor back into Miami Beach.

Travel in the city

Today's Miami is easily accessible to travelers within and beyond the US. Its international airport, welcoming some 24 million passengers each year is within a 15-minute drive of downtown and 25 minutes from Miami Beach. Greater Miami and the Beaches cover 1¼ million acres (½ million hectares); but the transportation system makes it relatively easy to get around. A rental car makes good sense since Miami attractions are widely scattered. (The regions are connected by major thoroughfares and causeways). Miami's elevated metrorail system runs from south of Dadeland Mall to downtown Miami, to northwest Dade County, and is connected to the downtown Metromover shuttle system. A flat-fare system includes free transfers between Metrorail and Metromover. Miami's port is large enough to accommodate the newest cruise ships. The port is easy to reach by bridge from downtown Miami's Bayfront Park, Biscayne Boulevard. A regular bus service operates into the city center.

What to look at

In every part of the city there is some new office block or resort hotel, and there are always plans for further development. Although downtown Miami has become an international business and financial hub, it is still attractive for visitors. Valuable acreage along Biscayne Bay remains parkland; Bayfront Park offers shady respite from urban bustle and honors prominent historic figures. This is the site of the John F. Kennedy Memorial Torch of Friendship, with its perpetual flame. And from Riverwalk you can see the glossy boats glinting in the sun.

Alternatively you can browse through Bayside with its speciality shops, marketplace and street entertainment. To the north, Bicentennial Park also fronts on to Biscayne Boulevard, providing a place to fish, bicycle and picnic. And in Mediterranean style Jose Marti Park, you can walk beside the Miami River, swim or relax. Miami's skyline is ever-changing: landmark monoliths include the 55-story Southeast Financial Center overlooking the Bay, and the 47-story Centrust office tower. Banks and high-rise condominiums shoot up along Brickell Avenue – some featuring circular staircases, jacuzzis and palm trees; some with a rooftop solarium, some rainbow-colored.

If the city has been investing in its future, so has The Beach, which stretches over 10 miles (16km) along the Atlantic and is as wide as a football field is long. Having emerged from a slump period, it can once again claim to have one of the

In less than 100 years Miami has grown to be a major business center

best and most exciting shorelines in the US. Walk along the beachfront promenade, a 2-mile (3km) boardwalk between 21st and 46th Streets, and you'll see what we mean.

Miami's marina is one of the best locations for all kinds of aquatic activities: charter dive boats and sailboats, powerboats and sportfishing boats, glass-bottom boat rides and much more. This is the place to watch the cruise ships; or you can listen to a concert in South Pointe Park where there are jetty promenades and observation towers, picnic pavilions and,

for the more energetic, a fitness course.

Everything in Miami seems either to be new or revived. In the 1950s the hotels along Collins Avenue became legendary, and now they have found new fame after being refurbished to meet the needs of the 1990s traveler. The Art Deco District at the southern end of The Beach is once more of interest, and its preserved 1930s hotels are enjoying a renaissance. A walking tour of the area, introduced in 1990, is a good way to get a feel for the days when American flappers strolled the sidewalks of Lincoln Road.

Although residents refer to The Beach, in fact there are several beaches, all communities with their own names. Surfside, for example, is wedged between Miami Beach to the south and Bal Harbour to the north. Accommodation is likely to cost less here, but Surfside sits by its own broad 1-mile (1.6km) beach and boasts a main shopping and dining area along Harding Avenue, bordered by flowers and palm trees. Bal Harbour is more prestigious, though less than a mile in size, with shops on a par with Rodeo Drive in Beverly Hills.

Just north of Haulover Park, a resort area with 3 miles (4.8km) of white sand beaches calls itself Sunny Isles, and has its own host of attractions for visitors, including outdoor activities, hotels and shopping malls.

Greater Miami is definitely international, as you will discover when sightseeing, dining or joining in the myriad festivities taking place all through the year. Bahamians who helped settle the village of Coconut Grove are the originators of the Miami Goombay Festival in June. Every March Little Havana hosts its own Hispanic festival – a Rio carnival in miniature. Haitians, too, have added their traditions to the Miami melting pot along with Germans (a resident Oktoberfest) and Italians (a resident Renaissance Fair – see **Festivals and Events**, pages 116-18).

WHAT TO SEE

AMELIA EARHART PARK
119th St and Lejeune Rd.
A new agricultural theme park named after the famous aviator who took off on her last flight from Miami. An interesting place to relax.

◆
ARCH CREEK PARK
NE 135th St and Biscayne Boulevard.
A different kind of museum in the northern section of Miami, containing artifacts of the prehistoric Tequesta Indians as well as million-year-old Mastodon bones. There are also live animals and nature displays, and nature walks are conducted most days. Admission is free.

◆◆◆
ART DECO DISTRICT
from 6th to 23rd St between Jefferson Ave and Miami Beach.
The only national historic district to be built in the 20th century. This district is where 800 or so buildings were designed in the art deco style and colors of the 1930s. Only 10 years ago, this area of The Beach was a neighborhood of run-down hotels with no upscale nightlife and only undistinguished eating places. But in 1986 14 hotels reopened their doors in restored splendor with sparkling decorative terrazzo floors, brass elevator doors and mirrored walls. Landmarks include the 70-room Cardozo, originally designed in 1939 and used in the 1950s for Frank Sinatra's

MIAMI

Miami's art deco hotels have been restored to their 1930s glory

film *A Hole in the Head*. Visitors to the district these days will find open air markets, Jewish delicatessens, excellent bakeries and Latin cafés. Along Ocean Drive, the Leslie Hotel with its SoBe Café is fully restored; the Carlyle Hotel and grill and the Waldorf Towers with its popular Downstairs at the Waldorf are again packing in the customers, along with the Breakwater Hotel and its rendezvous, Gerry's Place. Ovo Nightclub, at the corner of Espanola Way and Collins Avenue, once housed the Warsaw Ballroom. It now features gourmet cuisine and dancing. The old Cinema Theater on Washington Avenue was an art deco gem in its time. Caring renovation has given it new life, as Club 1235. Lincoln Road has been revived as a pedestrianized shopping mall, and the old Colony Theater, built as a showcase for Paramount Pictures in the 1930s, is now a modern performing arts center.

Espanola Way, a 1920s relic when fantasy themes were at their height, once again resembles the Spanish Village it was intended to be. Further development recently provided an oceanfront promenade, decorative paving, wider sidewalks and landscaping.

Art deco made its debut in Paris in 1925, but most impressed America in 1933 at the Chicago World's Fair. The Miami Design Preservation League conducts Saturday morning tours of the district for a small charge, and the Art

Deco Welcome Center conducts tours daily except Sunday, leaving from 661 Washington Avenue. Special events frequently take place in the neighborhood, such as the annual January Art Deco Weekend (see **Festivals and Events**, pages 116-18).

◆
BASS MUSEUM
2121 Park Avenue, Miami Beach.
This art gallery in the Art Deco District houses a permanent collection of medieval, Renaissance, baroque and rococo works, including Rubens, Lautrec and Van Haarlem. Closed Monday.

◆◆
BAYFRONT PARK
Biscayne Boulevard.
Vast improvements have recently been made to this bayside park, including an amphitheater which can seat 20,000 for outdoor concerts and other events. Panoramic views, picnic pavilions, and a café and restaurant add to the appeal of wide green spaces. The park incorporates a shopping and dining complex that surrounds the marina. From the marina, sightseeing boat and gondola rides are available and HMS Bounty (used in the original film *Mutiny on the Bounty*) is moored at Bayside. Magicians, strolling musicians and mimes frequently entertain here.

◆◆◆
CALLE OCHO
SW 8th St.
They call this 30-block strip "Little Havana" and it certainly reflects the influence of Cuban culture. This is the place to shop (even on a Sunday) for delicious pastries and sweet black coffee, to sample Latin cuisine and buy cigars. The small cigar factories where you can see the end-product being hand rolled are among the few places that actually thank you for smoking!
The neighborhood's Latin Quarter is Miami's answer to New Orleans' French Quarter. It combines shops and restaurants, flower stalls and strolling musicians, and stretches as far as 7th Street and 17th Avenue.
A fiesta air is always prevalent along Calle Ocho (Spanish for 8th Street), but no more so than every March when the entire Hispanic community throws a street party for everyone.

◆
CAULEY SQUARE
22400 Old Dixie Highway, Homestead.
This 10-acre historic railroad village is an example of typical 1920s Spanish style architecture. The two-story complex – a building of thick stucco walls and coral rock – now houses a variety of boutiques, art galleries and craft shops. It includes an ice cream parlor and children's party center, and is perhaps more designed for browsers than for serious shoppers. Annual festivals highlighting regional crafts and foods are held here every March, July and November.
Closed Sunday.

◆◆◆
COCONUT GROVE
Bird Rd (north), Le Jeune (west), Biscayne Bay (east) and Edgwater Drive (south).

Florida's fashionable answer to New York's Greenwich Village, San Francisco's Sausalito, or Washington's Georgetown. Only a 10-minute drive from downtown, the Grove is famous for its exclusive boutiques, restaurants and hotels. But perhaps best known is the Playhouse – a famous film theater for years and now the home of South Florida's leading resident professional theater company.

The district is lively and chic and has earned the adjective "Europeanized" with its sidewalk cafés, tiny bistros and pavement art shows. Shoppers should visit Mayfair-in-the-Grove, the Main Highway, Fuller Street, Grand Avenue and Commodore Plaza.

Nightclubs offer a great variety of sounds including jazz, country and western and reggae. They may well be tucked away in side streets and arcades, so it's worth exploring. Walking around the Grove is really the best way to discover the area, but a daily shuttle operates between Metrorail's Grove station and the hotels and attractions.

The **Barnacle** on the Main Highway is one place worth seeing. This was the home of Ralph Middleton Munroe, an early pioneer to the area, and is now a state historic site and museum, with beautifully landscaped grounds and a very low entrance fee.

Vizcaya and the **Museum of Science and Space Transit Planetarium** (see below) are also located in this district. Coconut Grove is a diverse and lively community, and can be seen at its best during festival times. The three-day February Arts Festival brings the crowds to the streets to see the artisans' work and taste the delicacies being offered. The June Goombay Festival is a Bahamian celebration; and the King Mango Strut in December is an "anything goes" jamboree. Sports are not forgotten either; at the Dinner Key Marina on the Bay, you can rent sailboats and windsurfers or charter fishing boats. This Key used to be Pan Am's seaplane landing base and terminal, and was exceptionally busy in the 1930s and 1940s.

Italianate splendor in the East Loggia of the Vizcaya mansion

CORAL CASTLE
28655 South Dixie Highway, Homestead.
A very strange but fascinating pile of rock, built between 1920 and 1940 by a Latvian immigrant for a woman who jilted him the day before they were to be married. He dug the 1,000 tons of coral for it single-handedly to build the outdoor furniture and solar-heated bathtubs. It is 25 miles (40km) south of Miami on US1.

CORAL GABLES
An elite residential district designed by George Merrick in the 1920s in Mediterranean style. Through coral rock gates and archways you may catch a glimpse of some of Miami's most desirable properties. Indeed, architectural standards are still strictly controlled to protect this garden area's beauty, and the boulevards, overlooked by leafy banyans, palms and poincianas, are well maintained.
It was in this area that the University of Miami was founded, and a variety of campus activities keeps the Gables lively. There is also good theater, first-class dining in restaurants which reflect the city's international air, and plenty of interesting shops, including those along the celebrated Miracle Mile. Bus tours are given of the Gables but it is equally easy to take the 20-mile (32km) self-guided tour prepared for visitors by the city; maps are free. If you decide to do so,

start at the gateway to the Gables, **La Puerta del Sol**. Merrick erected this 90ft (27m) belltower and 40ft (12m) arch and put it on the National Register of Historic Places. Among the district's attractions is Merrick's boyhood home, **Coral Gables House**, 907 Coral Way, for which the city was named; the house was originally constructed in 1898, of locally quarried coal. It is furnished in 1920s style, with many Merrick family pieces. Open Sunday and Wednesday afternoons only. Another "sight" in the city of Coral Gables is the **Venetian Pool**. This exotic lagoon is a natural spring-fed pool carved from coral rock in 1923 and enhanced with palms, islands, caves, waterfalls and arched bridges. Very popular with children in summer.
The Gables is not lacking in museums. **Lowe Art Museum**, located on the University campus, is the county's oldest for visual arts and is distinguished by its Kress collection of Old Masters. The collections of southwest American Native art and textiles are worth seeing, too (closed Monday).

Fairchild Gardens (see page 18) are also worth visiting, and a novel way to tour the district is to rent a bicycle and take advantage of the miles of special bike paths which loop through shaded streets down the Old Cutler Road Bikeway to Matheson Hammock Country Park. Coral Gables is close to downtown.

MIAMI

◆◆
FAIRCHILD TROPICAL GARDENS
Old Cutler Rd, Coral Gables.
A favorite stop on most itineraries, these gardens are said to have the country's largest subtropical botanical variety, with over 80 acres of palms, cycads and other exotic plants from around the world. You can take the winding paths through a rain forest, the Vine Pergola, Sunken Garden, Palm Glade and Rare Plant House and around eight lakes, or opt for one of the guided tram tours. Children under 13 accompanying their parents do not have to pay an entrance fee.

◆
FLAMINGO PARK
1245 Michigan Ave, Miami Beach.
This is the place for tennis lovers. The tennis complex comprises clay and hard courts, many of them lit for night playing, and tournaments are frequently held in the 5,000-seat Abel Holtz Stadium. There are also other recreational facilities on offer here, including a swimming pool.

◆
FREEDOM TOWER
600 Biscayne Boulevard.
Inspired by the Giralda Tower in Spain, this structure was built in 1925 to house the Miami Daily News. It changed its name in the 1960s when it became the Cuban Refugee Emergency Center. Open to the public.

◆
FRUIT AND SPICE PARK
24801 SW 187th Avenue, Homestead.
An unusual botanical park, featuring, as its name suggests, fruits and spices from around the globe – more than 200 species and 500 varieties, on 20 acres. Of particular interest is the demonstration herb and vegetable garden. Admission is free for those who want to tour on their own but a small charge is made for a guided tour (weekends only). It is 35 miles (56km) southwest of Miami off US1.

◆
GOLD COAST RAILROAD & MUSEUM
12450 SW 152nd St.
An operating railway museum whose displays include presidential cars, steam and diesel locomotives. Visitors may also take the 3½-mile (5km) half-hour trip on a 1913 steam train.

A vivid Bird of Paradise flower in the Fairchild Tropical Gardens

MIAMI AND MIAMI BEACH

◆
HAULOVER PARK
10800 Collins Ave.
This major recreational park is a popular spot for surfing, and has an ocean-front pier for fishing and a marina where boats may be rented. It also includes a nine-hole golf course.

HIALEAH

Okeechobee Rd.

The Miami Canal separates this sporting district from its sister city, Miami Springs. The Hialeah Racetrack is one of the biggest draws, though people like to visit its park site outside the racing season to enjoy the superbly landscaped grounds. An aquarium, aviary and a flock of uncaged flamingos add to the attraction. Another reason to visit Hialeah is the Miami Jai-Alai Fronton the country's oldest and largest arena for the very popular old Basque game, where a *pelota* (a very hard ball) is hurtled around a court at speeds of up to 150mph. It is enjoyed by spectators who can bet on teams or individual players, or merely watch the action over dinner in the clubhouse.

◆

KENNEDY PARK

South Bayshore Drive and Kirk St, Coconut Grove.

Popular with joggers or for a work-out on the Vita course; and just for fun there's a frisbee golf course.

KEY BISCAYNE

This somewhat secluded island is the first of the arc of small islands that form The Keys, but as it is only a bridge away from the city and The Beach, it is very much a part of Miami. In the 1940s, when the causeway was constructed, urban dwellers began to realize the potential of this island as a weekend retreat. Today there are private homes, hotels, business operations and many sports facilities in a setting of lush foliage.

At one end of the island, **Crandon Park** is favored by golfers and picnickers. At the southern tip of Key Biscayne, the smaller **Bill Baggs Cape Florida State Recreation Area** is also an area for outdoor enjoyment. Here, Cape Florida Lighthouse was built in 1825, and now houses a historical museum. It is south Florida's oldest landmark, survivor of both the Seminole Wars and the Civil War. Don't miss a visit to America's largest aquatic park, **Biscayne National Underwater Park**. A glass-bottomed boat is the only way to explore 181 acres (73 hectares) of colorful reefs, home to numerous species of tropical fish; but you can leave the boat to snorkel or scuba dive. **Virginia Key**, an island just north of Key Biscayne, is where you will find the **Miami Marine Stadium**, site of international rowing events and summer pop concerts. Also here is the **Miami Seaquarium**. Reach both islands on Rickenbacker Causeway.

LUMMUS PARK

between 5th and 14th St, Miami Beach.

Beach concerts here are free and you can rent umbrellas and watersports equipment in this grassy, palm-lined park next to the beach. Another Lummus Park is situated in the middle of the downtown

Windsurfing is popular on Key Biscayne, part of The Keys and of Miami

Government Center, where the old Wagner Building has been restored, and is the site of the Fort Dallas barracks.

MALIBU GRAND PRIX
NW 8th St.
A family park that features miniature golf, go-carts, batting cages, video games arcades, plus formula and sprint racing cars. Free admission, separate fees for each attraction. Open late.

METRO-DADE CULTURAL CENTER
101 West Flagler St.
If the weather is dull, this complex in the heart of downtown might be the place to visit. Built in a Mediterranean style around a plaza 14ft (4m) above Flagler Street, it covers a city block and embraces a library and two museums. Entrance to the **Center for the Fine Arts** is by covered walkway from the central plaza. In addition to an auditorium and exhibition space, there are two floors of main galleries and a sculpture court, including The Great Horse by Raymond Duchamp-Villon. Closed Monday.
In the **Historical Museum of Southern Florida** you will find hands-on exhibits which tell the 10,000-year story of humans in this region.

METROZOO
Coral Reef Drive and SW 124th Ave.
Miami's zoo is one of the most modern cageless varieties,

allowing some 100 species, including white tigers and rhinos, to roam at will through 225 acres (90 hectares) of near-natural habitats, separated from visitors by moats. Wings of Asia is a free-flight aviary with 300 tropical birds.
Monorail tours give an overall view, but boats and elephants are also available as transportation, and the petting zoo is ideal for small children. Take the Florida Turnpike or US1 to SW 152nd Street and follow the signs.

MIAMI SEAQUARIUM
Virginia Key, via Rickenbacker Causeway.
Highly recommended for children, who can spend an action-packed day here. Dolphins, sealions and killer whales all have starring roles in shows given several times a day. Tanks display rare

Dolphins at the Miami Seaquarium

tropical fish; there are tropical gardens and a wildlife sanctuary.

MIAMI YOUTH MUSEUM
Bakery Center, 5701 Sunset Dr.
This hands-on cultural arts center is designed to encourage youngsters to appreciate art by creating their own visual and musical effects. Admission free for under 4s.

◆
MICCOSUKEE INDIAN VILLAGE
Tamiami Station.
Aimed primarily at tourists; children will no doubt appreciate the alligator wrestling, even if they are not interested in the exhibits of tribal patchwork and basketry. Take US41; about 30 miles (48km) west of Miami.

MONKEY VILLAGE
14805 SW 216th St, South Miami.
Here you can walk along a caged pathway through a near-natural rain forest, while the monkeys swing free. They have even more avid curiosity than their visitors, and their antics are highly entertaining. Gorillas, orangutans and the tiniest monkeys can be seen, but the stars are clever chimps. Recommended for children. Admission free for under 5's. Reached via US1.

MUSEUM OF SCIENCE AND SPACE TRANSIT PLANETARIUM
3280 S Miami Ave, Coconut Grove.

An educational museum which manages to be fun; this one explores the worlds of light, sound, energy, biology and much more. Over 100 hands-on exhibits and computer games. Multimedia and laser shows are given in the planetarium and, weather permitting, star gazing is free on weekend evenings in the Weintraub Observatory. Also look in at the Animal Exploratorium, where reptiles and local marine life may be handled. Recommended for children.

◆
ORCHID JUNGLE
26715 SW 157th Ave, Homestead.
This natural Florida jungle is where the loveliest of orchids from around the world grow. Wander at will along one of the jungle trails. 25 miles (40km) south of Miami; reached via US1.

◆◆◆
PARROT JUNGLE AND GARDENS
11000 SW 57th Ave.
Perennial favorite and one of Florida's oldest and best developed attractions. Hundreds of brilliantly colored tropical birds fly around, often perching on your shoulder, but there are also 2,000 varieties of plants and flowers growing here. One highlight is the trained bird show in the Parrot Bowl, when cockatoos and macaws do a high-wire act, skate and perform a number of other tricks. After the show, stay for the parade of pink flamingos. Recommended for children; under 6's free.

SOUTH POINTE PARK
Government Cut.
This 17-acre (7-hectare) park, at the southern end of Miami Beach, has exercise courses, play areas for children, observation towers, picnic areas, an amphitheater for concerts and a restaurant.

◆◆
SPANISH MONASTERY
North Miami Beach.
If it looks authentically Spanish, it should: It was first erected in Spain in the 15th century, and brought piecemeal to America in 1954. The monastery of St Bernard houses antiques and works of art. Open to the public.

◆◆◆
VIZCAYA
3251 South Miami Ave, Coconut Grove.
Once the home of James Deering, founder of International Harvester, this 70-room Italianate mansion sits in 10 acres of formal gardens overlooking Biscayne Bay. Lavishly decorated, it is a treasure house of European art. The Shakespeare Festival and Italian Renaissance Fair are both held on the grounds.

◆
WEEKS AIR MUSEUM
14710 SW 128th St, Tamiami Airport.
A museum dedicated to the preservation of aircraft from their beginnings through World War II. More than 35 aircraft (many restored to flying condition) are on display.

Accommodations

There is a multitude of world class hotels, tourist priced hotels and holiday apartments in the Miami area. For some of the chains (*eg.,* Howard Johnsons) it is possible to prepurchase accommodations coupons. For central reservation service call (800) 950 0232, toll free.

The following are some recommended hotels in the top bracket:

Alexander All-Suite Luxury Hotel, 5225 Collins Ave, Miami Beach (tel: (305) 865 6500). Interesting and plush hotel where all 206 rooms are suites with their own kitchen. Hotel facilities include dining room, cocktail lounge, entertainment, room service, pools, tennis courts and golf course privileges. A splendid oceanfront property within a 15-minute drive of the airport for anyone who can afford the rates.

Biscayne Bay Marriott Hotel & Marina, 1633 N. Bayshore Drive (tel: (305) 374 3900). A downtown bayfront 605-room hotel connected by skywalk to Omni International Shopping Mall. Choice of three restaurants and lounges, pool, sauna and whirlpool and complimentary transportation to the airport.

Doral Ocean Beach Resort, 4833 Collins Ave, Miami Beach (tel: (305) 532 3600). Long established and revived 420-room beachfront hotel. Guest rooms are delightful, if costly, as are the dining room and pleasant coffee shop. Other facilities available are gardens, pool, tennis courts and aqua club, and a golf course at the Doral Resort & Country Club near the airport.

Fontainebleau Hilton Resort, 4441 Collins Ave, Miami Beach (tel: (305) 538 2000). Enormous but beautifully laid out, long established beachfront hotel with 1,206 rooms. Landscaping includes rock grotto freeform pool. There are 14 restaurants and lounges to choose from, including *al fresco*, and a nightclub where many top names perform. Sports facilities include tennis.

Grand Bay Hotel, 2669 S. Bayshore Drive, Coconut Grove (tel: (305) 858 9600). Plush 181-room European style hotel overlooking Biscayne Bay in attractive garden setting. Special touches include 24-hour room service and lots of fresh flowers. With 181 rooms, this is more intimate than most. Facilities include health club, pool, sauna and whirlpool, elegant restaurant and prestigious Regine's nightclub.

Sheraton Bal Harbour, 9701 Collins Ave (tel: (305) 865 7511). A 675-room hotel in a glamorous beachfront location. Rooms have kitchenettes. Nine restaurants and lounges, and a supper club noted for musical revues. Other facilities include two pools, sauna, whirlpool and tennis.

In the Art Deco District, several smallish hotels have been restored and are particularly popular: notably the **Carlyle**, 1250 Ocean Dr (tel: (305) 532 5315); **Waldorf**

Tower, 860 Ocean Dr (tel: (305) 531 7684); **Edison**, 960 Ocean Dr (tel: (305) 531 0461); and **Park Central**, 640 Ocean Dr (tel: (305) 538 1611).
In Sunny Isles, reasonably priced hotels include **Chateau-By-The-Sea** and **Driftwood Resort Motel**, 17121 Collins Ave (tel: (305) 944 5141). Also recommended in this area are the **Marco Polo**, 19201 Collins Ave (tel: (305) 932 2233); and **Radisson Pan-American Hotel**, 17875 Collins Ave (tel: (305) 932 1100). **Mayfair House**, Florida Ave, Coconut Grove (tel: (305) 441 0000), is rather unusual; all 185 suites feature their own jacuzzi and often an upright (antique) piano. **The Biltmore** (Biscayne Bay), which dates from 1926, has been restored and is closed at present, possibly opening in the autumn of 1991. **The Inter-Continental**, 100 Chopin Plaza (tel: (800) 332 4246 toll free),

has a permanent collection of priceless tapestries.
Sheraton Royal Biscayne Beach Resort & Racquet Club, 555 Ocean Drive, Key Biscayne (tel: (305) 361 5775). Glamorous oceanfront resort with its own private beach. Good sport facilities include two pools and ten tennis courts.

Children
Many family attractions in the Miami area are ideal for children. Novel animal shows are presented at both Monkey and Parrot Jungles and, of course, the dolphins and whales are the stars at Miami Seaquarium. Exotic species can be seen at the Metrozoo. Of special note among a variety of museums are the Museum of Science and Space Transit Planetarium, and the Miami Youth Museum (see **What to see**).

A flock of flamingos in the pink at Parrot Jungle

Restaurants

When it comes to eating in Miami you're truly spoiled for choice. A vast range of ethnic cuisine is available, and fast food outlets are innumerable. (Consult *The Greater Miami Menu Guide*, a dining and entertainments listing from newsstands and certain hotels.) Among the hotel restaurants recommended are:

Dominique's, Alexander Hotel, 5225 Collins Ave, Miami Beach (tel: (305) 865 6500). Considered romantic and excellent. The pink and green dining room is enhanced by Oriental rugs and antique furniture; menu is French.

Restaurant Place St Michel, Hotel Place St Michel, 162 Alcazar Ave, Coral Gables (tel: (305) 444 1666). A café atmosphere for French cuisine, breakfast, lunch and dinner. Good Sunday brunch with a champagne buffet.

Veronique's, Biscayne Bay Marriott, 1633 North Bayshore Drive (tel: (305) 374 3900). Gourmet setting for *haute cuisine* and local seafood. First class (and expensive) service includes at-table presentations. Nonhotel restaurants worth looking at include:

Casa Juancho, 2436 SW 8th St (tel: (305) 642 2452). In the heart of Miami's Spanish district, this upscale restaurant features regional Spanish cuisine, plus Tapas menu, and strolling musicians in 14th-century outfits. Jacket and tie required.

Chart House Restaurant, 51 Chart House Drive, Coconut Grove (tel: (305) 856 9741). Features thick steak and tender prime rib, oysters and seafood dishes; there is also an outstanding salad bar. Cut costs by sticking to cocktails and appetizers on one of the outside decks overlooking Biscayne Bay.

Dockside Terrace, Bayside Marketplace, 401 Biscayne Blvd (tel: (305) 359 6419). Casual waterfront spot with a good view of the Marketplace and marina. Seafood is a speciality indoors or out on the terrace.

East Coast Fisheries Restaurant, 360 W Flagler St (tel: (305) 373 5515). Long established seafood restaurant on the Miami River. The first floor doubles as fish market and dining room so you can be sure the seafood is fresh.

Joe's Stone Crab, 227 Biscayne Blvd, Miami Beach (tel: (305) 673 0365). Something of an evergreen, this has been operating since 1913. Large, noisy and casual; the seafood is delicious. If the stone crabs are in season, pick a platter of them, to be dipped in butter or mustard sauce. Closed mid-May to mid-October and Sunday and Monday lunchtime.

Euro Pub, 790 NE 79th St (tel: (305) 754 2678). Cosy, European-style inn with traditional dishes from Ireland, France, Italy, Austria, Hungary and Germany.

Shopping

Elegant speciality shops, indoor and outdoor malls – or shopping centers – and markets can be found all over Miami. There's a wonderful variety, including

Shopping is a speciality in Miami; Bayside Marketplace is a new center

neighborhood and ethnic shops as well as designer boutiques and discount areas. Below is a selection of the best and most interesting places for visitors to see – even if only to enjoy the surroundings and window-shop:

Aventura Mall, 19501 Biscayne Blvd, North Miami Beach. Expansive two-level mall with over 200 stores and 21 restaurants. In addition to boutiques and antique stores, there are major department stores such as Macy's and Lord & Taylor. Aventura is most easily reached from Dade and Broward counties.

Arthur Godfrey Road, east of the Julia Tuttle Causeway. The main thoroughfare from the airport to The Beach is one of the main shopping streets, easily reached on foot from many of the beachfront hotels. It is an old street but a flourishing one.

Bakery Center, South Miami. Multimillion dollar complex with many fine speciality stores, international restaurants and movie theaters. Unusual artwork surrounds it, including Jonathan Borofsky's 24ft (7m) Hammering Man and illusionary murals by Richard Haas.

Bal Harbour Shops, Collins Ave at 97th St. An exclusive shopping area in a beautifully designed garden setting with blossoming orange trees, tropical foliage and ferns. Saks Fifth Avenue and Neiman-Marcus are the department store anchors to this three-level open-air mall.

Bayside Marketplace, 401 Biscayne Blvd. The city's newest attraction: a two-story speciality center which encompasses 140 shops, restaurants and pavilions surrounding Miamarina at

Biscayne Bay. Look out particularly for shops selling fashions, handicrafts and Latin American food stalls.

Cutler Ridge Mall, 20505 S Dixie Highway, Cutler Ridge. Over 170 shops, including major department stores such as Lord & Taylor, Burdines, Jordan Marsh.

Dadeland Mall, 7535 N Kendall Drive, Kendall. Popular and busy. Anchor department stores are Jordan Marsh, Burdines, Saks Fifth Avenue and Lord & Taylor, but there are also speciality shops. Metrorail stops conveniently nearby.

The Falls, 8888 Howard Drive, Kendall. An outdoor mall with landscaped walkways, waterfalls and bridges, featuring a range of speciality shops and restaurants. Stores include Miami's only Bloomingdale's.

Flagler Street, downtown. A bustling street at the heart of the city with all types of shops, including Burdines.

Hallandale Flea Market, Gulfstream Race Track and Hallandale Beach Blvd. A good place to browse for new and secondhand goods; but it's only open at weekends.

Lincoln Road Mall, 16th St and Lincoln Rd, Miami Beach. Once the most popular place to shop, until all the others came along. Still holding its own, the mall has 175 stores lining an open-air pedestrianized zone where only electric trams operate. This mall is sometimes referred to as the

International Market Place.

Little Havana, SW 8th St (Calle Ocho) and W Flagler St. Sells all things Cuban. Look particularly for cigars.

Loehmann's Plaza, Biscayne Blvd at 187th St, North Miami Beach. Discount stores are a feature particularly worth looking for, selling extras in designer labels.

The Mall at 163rd St, North Miami Beach. Three-level complex boasting around 150 speciality shops as well as major department stores such as Burdines and Jordan Marsh.

Mayfair in the Grove, 2911 Grand Ave, Coconut Grove. Exclusive atrium-styled promenade where you can find the likes of Yves St Laurent and Ralph Lauren fashions, as well as elite restaurants and nightclubs to choose from.

Miami Fashion District, NW 5th Ave, and 22nd St. Shops featuring clothes and home accessories.

Miracle Mile, SW 24th St, Coral Gables. Almost anything you might want is to be found in the 150 or so stores along this tree-lined thoroughfare. Miracle Center has 50 specialist shops, a cinema, restaurants and nightclubs.

Omni International Mall, 1601 Biscayne Blvd. Part of a downtown hotel and convention facility, this five-floor enclosed mall has numerous speciality shops, exclusive boutiques, department stores and a variety of restaurants. A covered walkway links the Omni International Mall to the Biscayne Bay Marriott Hotel.

THE KEYS

The Keys are very special.
This group of 45 islands, which
the Spanish called *cayos*, is
dotted in a 150-miles (240km)
arc from the southern tip of the
mainland deep into the Gulf of
Mexico. Actually, early
explorers never stopped at
any of the rocky outcrops, but
referred to them as *Los
Martires*, or "The martyrs,"
because they looked like
suffering men rising from the
sea. The Native American
inhabitants were left to hunt
and fish in peace. In the 15th
century they would have been
from the fierce Calusa tribe,
but mounds still visible these
days suggest the earliest
residents were the Arawaks
and Caribees.
Pirates came and went and
sometimes wrecked but it
wasn't until the 18th century
that white settlers came to stay.
For the most part they farmed
– limes, tamarind and
breadfruit, and in the Lower
Keys, pineapples. Later, a
thriving shark factory was
established on Big Pine Key;
the shark hides were sent
north to be processed into a
tough leather known as
shagreen. Transplanted British
loyalists and Yankee seafarers
both arrived in the 19th
century, followed by Cubans,
who established cigar factories
there.
It was only during this century
that tourism reached The Keys.
Once Henry Flagler extended
his railroad from Miami to Key
West in 1912, the wealthy
were eager to enjoy the Keys'

*One of the world's longest cause-
ways links the Florida Keys*

good climate and relaxed
atmosphere. The railway was
supplanted by an "over-sea"
highway in 1938 – a
tremendous engineering feat
now incorporating 42 bridges,
including the well-known
Seven Mile Bridge. Travelers
by road can reach Key West
from Miami in three hours. It is
possible to fly there, but it
would be a shame to miss the
scenery: blue lagoons, olive
groves, white pines; herons,
spoonbills, pelicans and
osprey; and the unmatched
waters surrounding the islands
– the perfect location for
fishing, diving, sailing and
boating.

WHAT TO SEE

◆◆◆
KEY LARGO

This is the most northerly of the Keys, and is best known for **John Pennekamp Coral Reef State Park**, America's first underwater park, covering an area of some 75 square miles (194sq km) and accessible from Miami in about an hour's drive. Named after a Miami newspaper editor and conservationist, Pennekamp is a wonder for anyone with an interest in marine life. The waters are renownedly clear and calm; the underwater living world exotic and colorful. There are said to be almost 400 species of fish and over 40 different varieties of coral, as well as many other marine creatures.

There are four main ways to view Pennekamp, of which the glass-bottom boat is the easiest. Passengers are taken on a tour of Molasses Reef at the southern end of the park. This is also the most popular diving and snorkeling spot, for almost every kind of coral can be seen in one place.

Snorkeling can be done easily by anyone who can swim and a special boat leaves several times daily for 2½-hour reef trips, much of which time is actually spent in the water. A package price includes equipment and instruction. Alternatively, you can opt for a personalized snorkeling tour, with groups or no more than six people.

To join the dive boat, you do need to be a certified diver,

Humphrey Bogart's haunt in Key Largo was the Key's Caribbean Club

though scuba instruction is available. Dive sites vary depending upon conditions but are likely to be Molasses Reef, French Reef or Benwood Wreck. For human-made sights, try Dry Rocks, where a bronze statue of Christ is immersed in 20ft (6m) of water. The Jules Undersea Lodge provides overnight accommodations five fathoms below – write to POB 3330, Key Largo, FL 33037 for details.

Visitors looking for alternatives to the underwater attractions will find human-made beaches, canoe trails, nature trails and windsurfers for rent.

In October, Sands Key, Elliott Key and Old Rhodes Key in the Biscayne Waterway are the focal points for the annual

Columbus Day regatta. The tiny island between Elliott Key and Old Rhodes Key was once a pirate's stronghold known as Black Caesar's Rock. According to legend, Black Caesar was an escaped African-American slave who pirated ships so well singlehandedly that he became Blackbeard's trusty aide.

THE UPPER KEYS

Anywhere in this stretch of archipelago between Key Largo and Long Key is very easy to reach by car from Miami. You may care to stop at **Tavernier Key**; ornithologists tour the Florida Bay Rookeries from here.

The island's name comes from pirate Jean Lafitte's associate Tavernier, who frequently used it as a hiding place in the 18th century. Many historic

buildings have recently been restored.

◆◆
ISLAMORADA

An important and popular Upper Keys base in the center of a coral and palm-fringed group of islands colloquially known as "the purple isles," comprising Plantation, Windley, Upper and Lower Matecumbe Keys and Long Quay. "Purple" may refer to the concentration of violet sea snails (*Janthina Janthina*) found on the seashore here; though some say it is for the little wild flower that covers the islands in mulberry shades. There are first class resorts, marinas, tennis and golf facilities at Islamorada – one of the first areas to provide a nature walk and bicycle pathway for tourists. This is an excellent place to snorkel and scuba at the offshore **Coral Underwater Sea Garden**. It also has a reputation for being one of the finest fishing areas for tarpon and sailfish. Don't miss **Theater of the Sea** here; where porpoises and sea lions cavort in large, coral rock-lined natural ponds. A "Swim with a Dolphin" program allows you to jump in with these fascinating marine animals (tel: (305) 664 2431 to verify). You should also be able to see barracuda, shark and other, smaller reed dwellers. The purple isles were a notable wreckers' headquarters in the early years of the 19th century, and there is a wreck of a Spanish galleon off the coast. Tiny **Lignumvitae Key** is where some of the last remaining examples of the Key's original vegetation still grow. On this 280-acre island there are several Lignumvitae ("wood of life") trees along with mahogany, strangler fig, poisonwood, pigeon plum and gumbo limbo trees. This is now a state park botanic site, with conducted tours. **Long Key** is recommended for snorkelers. Dive shops will arrange individual or group trips to the nearby reefs. In the town of Layton there are **Zane Grey Creek** and **Sea World Shark Institute** to explore, and there are nature trails in **Long Key State Recreation Area**.

THE MIDDLE KEYS

The section of the archipelago between Long Key and the Seven Mile Bridge mostly consists of small island names like Conch, Duck, Crawl and Grassy – the latter being named after an early settler, not the vegetation. **Marathon** is a well developed tourist center in the Middle Keys, with its own airport, convention center and golf course. In earlier times, it was an escape hatch for such pirates as Morgan and Lafitte. On **Grassy Key** there's a **Dolphin Research Center** where the dolphins live in a natural environment, and educational tours inform the public about their lifestyle, or visitors can encounter them more closely by going swimming with them (tel: (305) 289 1121).

THE LOWER KEYS

This is the area between The Seven Mile Bridge and Key West; largest of these Keys is:

BIG PINE KEY

Covered with silver palmetto, Caribbean pine and cacti, this tropical islet lies a few miles from Key West and is most famous for its handful of tiny deer (little bigger than an average-sized dog) which once were plentiful throughout the Keys. Nowadays, the few that are left are virtually confined to Big Pine Key, and protected in the National Key Deer Refuge. If you see one, don't feed it.

Six miles (9½km) south of Big Pine Key is **Looe Key National Marine Sanctuary**, a magnificent coral reef providing an ideal spot for snorkeling and diving in anything from 2 to 40ft of warm, clear Gulf Stream water. Access is by boat from the Bahia Honda State Recreation Area.

KEY WEST

The most southerly Key and the best known. It boasts the most opulent resorts, most familiar personalities, most obviously colorful history and the most lively nightlife. The smugglers and the rum-runners loved it in the past, and a diverse set of people love it today. Perhaps the best time to come is festival time.

In October the Fantasy Fest embraces Hallowe'en and is Key West's answer to the *mardi gras*, with street fairs, arts and crafts shows, parades and floats and food *fests*.

February brings the excitement of Old Island Days. At this time of year, private homes are lit up, and some of their owners invite the general public inside; fun and games include a conch shell blowing contest, and many other festivities, which finish in March with the blessing of the local shrimp fleet. Although this celebration was only launched in 1960, it has become extremely popular; area captains now paint their vessels and deck them out with bunting for the occasion.

Summer visitors should make a note that the anniversary of former resident Ernest Hemingway's birth is 21 July, and this is commemorated with a week-long festival. A look-alike contest, short story and story telling contests, costume party and billfish tournament (a deep-sea fishing contest) are all included in what Key West calls Hemingway Days.

Hemingway loved Key West and Hemingway House on Whitehead Street is now a museum, housing photographs and other memorabilia, including his typewriter and descendants of his cats. Occasionally visitors are guided around the house by friends of the author. The swimming pool here was the first in Key West.

Across the street is the **Lighthouse Military Museum**. Here visitors may climb to the top, peer through a submarine periscope and wander through half an acre of military hardware. Displays include one of the two remaining "two man"

Ernest Hemingway's Key West home

submarines launched by the Imperial Japanese Navy during World War II.

Audubon House on Whitehead Street is where the noted artist and naturalist John James Audubon stayed when he visited the Keys in 1832. A well restored 1812 mansion, it was the home of salvager and harbor pilot Captain John Geiger, and is furnished in the period's style. Numerous original Audubon engravings are on view, many from his famous Birds of America folio. During his visits Audubon explored the mangroves in search of native birds, often starting out at 3:00 A.M.. You can take a guided tour or watch a video, showing the tremendous detail of his drawings.

Oldest House (Wreckers Museum) is located on Duval

Street, the best shopping and dining street. It is an 1829 sea captain's house, with the ship's hatch in the roof showing the influence of early shipbuilding. Many early "gingerbread" style houses, with railings and large verandas, were built by ships' carpenters. Inside there are models of shops and a furnished dolls' house.

There are several good restaurants along Duval Street, often in courtyard settings. But the main rendezvous point is **Mallory Square** by the waterfront – especially at sunset. If you haven't seen a Mallory Pier sunset you haven't lived, they say, and at this time of day the square really comes alive: tumblers, jugglers, string quartets – and all free.

Here, too, is the **Key West Aquarium**, the first open-air aquarium to be built in the US and the first attraction for the Keys. You can see a living coral reef, shark tanks and a turtle pool. The "touch tank" contains creatures which may safely be handled.

Turtle Kraals is in the shrimp dock area and is home to loggerhead turtles weighing up to 400 pounds (180kg). There is also a "touch tank" for children and an aviary.

Mel Fisher Maritime Heritage Society's Treasure Museum on Greene Street displays millions of dollars worth of treasure – gold and silver bars and jewelery. They were retrieved by Fisher from the wreck of the *Atocha*, which sank in 1622.

President Harry Truman's former winter home in Key West, just beyond the western end of Southard Street, is known as the **Little White House**. It was remodeled for him after his first visit to Key West in 1946, and it was here, two years later, that he held the famous conference of joint chiefs-of-staff to plan the unification of the armed forces. Restored to its earlier appearance, the house opened to the public in 1991.

A recent Key West attraction is **Fort Zachary Taylor Historic Site**. Fort Taylor, a preCivil War relic, recalls a time when Union troops occupied the city. Though the remainder of Florida was a firm part of the Confederacy, the Union flag flew over this fort and prevented a takeover by the Rebels. Part of the recreational section includes a pleasant beachfront. Another of the island's fortifications, East Martello Tower, now houses a historical museum and art gallery.

If there is one typical Key West sport, it's fishing. A variety of sportfishing is available almost any time of the year – Atlantic Ocean reefs, Gulfstream big-game angling and the Gulf of Mexico and backwaters. A day's deep-sea fishing off the Key West boat docks is a memorable experience. Less ambitious fishermen will find their challenge in the natural coral reefs and among the many shipwrecks in Key West waters. Younger fishermen can enjoy saltwater fishing, at a minimal cost.

One of the notable sights of a tiny isle: Key West's White Church

Since the island city of Key West is a mere 3½ by 1 mile (5½ by 1½km) in size, getting around is simple. You don't even need a car to see most of it, but if you would rather not walk, take an Old Town Trolley tour which offers transportation to and from hotels and gives narrated tours of the historic landmarks, including the old Navy docks, with a climb up Solaris Hill, the city's highest point. You can leave the tour at any stop and rejoin it later. A popular alternative is the Conch Tour Train, comprising small, open canopied cars.

Accommodations

There are lodges, b&bs and hotels throughout the Keys, most plentiful in Islamorada and Key West. **Cheeca Lodge** is a good choice in the former. **The Reach** is just outside the latter. **Marriotts Casa Marina Resort** and **Pier House** are both recommended. Many Key West b&bs are in charming old houses; camping areas are prolific in the Lower Keys.

Children

Any children who are water babies or can throw a fishing line will love the Keys; dress is casual and evening activities finish early. Most enjoyment is in John Pennekamp State Park (Key Largo), Islamorada and Key West.

Restaurants

The most chic restaurants are in Key West, but there is no shortage of places to eat good seafood: shrimp, of course, and red snapper, tiny grunts and stone crabs. Look for oyster bars and menus which feature conch and clams. A number of restaurants favor Cuban and Bahamian cuisine but other ethnic restaurants have recently been established. Well-known restaurants in Key West include **Louie's Backyard**, 700 Waddell Ave (tel: (305) 294 1061), **Harbor Lights**, Garrison Bight Causeway (tel: (305) 294 9343) and **Bagatelle**, 115 Duval Street (tel: (305) 296 6604).

Shopping

Most of the shops are in Key West, where there are street stalls, smart boutiques and many more. Local souvenir shops elsewhere sell naturally sculpted driftwood, coconut products and straw items. Most are to be found along Duval Street, and around Mallory Square which has a market.

A tranquil setting for sunset fishing on the Florida Keys

LEE ISLAND COAST

The Lee Island Coast is an area of Florida not widely known by tourists. Of its islands, many are still undisturbed or barely inhabited; some are only accessible by boat. Their names alone are evocative: Sanibel, Captiva, Estero, Pine, Cayo Costa, Punta Blanca, Cayo Pelau, Buck and Devilfish Keys, Johnson Shoals and Chino Island. This is a coast with a Caribbean aura, offering pristine secluded beaches and marvelous sunsets; but within easy reach of the "City of Palms," Fort Myers.

Although the weather here is good all year round, you'll get the best values between Easter and mid-December, which Lee County calls its "Secret Season." Here in southwest Florida, with its hundreds of offshore barrier islands, there is less development, but accommodations are plentiful, and reasonably priced.

This is the perfect location for boaters; there are around 25 marinas in the area, where you can rent a simple motor boat or part of a fully-fledged sailing flotilla. Conditions are always good, and the boating byways meeting here include the Intracoastal Waterway, Okeechobee Waterway and the Gulf of Mexico.

Beachcombers are unlikely to find all the shells strewn along the scenic beaches; there are over 400 species, including tulips, olives, paper figs and junonia. This section of the state also lays claim to nature sanctuaries covering thousands of acres. Among the best are the J N "Ding" Darling National Wildlife Refuge, the Sanibel-Captiva Conservation Foundation, the Lee County Nature Center, **Carl E Johnson Park** (see below), Matanzas Pass Wilderness Preserve, Mound Key and Cayo Costa State Island Preserve.

WHAT TO SEE

BLACK ISLAND

If for no other reason, come here for a delightful picnic at Lover's Key in **Carl E Johnson Park**. Visitors are driven by tram across scenic mangrove islands to reach the picturesque beach. There is a snack bar, canoes for rent and nature trails through the park. Black Island lies just south of Estero Island.

BONITA BEACH

Occupying the southern boundary of the Lee Island Coast, Bonita Beach (between Fort Myers Beach and Bonita Springs) is probably one of the west coast's most superb beaches. There are shops and restaurants (many with waterfront views) here as well as some cottage style and condominium accommodations. On the active side, there's greyhound racing at the Naples/Fort Myers Kennel Club in Bonita Springs between October and early August, and Imperial River, one of Bonita Springs' most precious natural resources, is said to offer the best canoeing in the area. You could take the children to **Golf Safari** on Bonita Beach Road, where waterfalls and tropical gardens are the setting for an 18-hole miniature golf course – or to **Everglades Wonder Gardens** in Bonita Springs (one of the state's first attractions), native and exotic wildlife.

◆
CABBAGE ISLAND

Just the place for the island dreamer who doesn't want to be completely deserted. Life is quiet here but the company is usually interesting at the tiny inn which used to be part of the estate of mystery writer Mary Roberts Rinehart. The inn only has six guest rooms but it does have a very popular dining room papered with autographed dollar bills – worth around $10,000 to date if it were all taken down! It has become a custom for first-time visitors to follow the tradition. **Cabbage Key** is built on top of an ancient Caloosa Indian shell mound – one of the highest elevations in the southwest. There are nature trails to explore, a water tower to climb for a panoramic view of Pine Island Sound, and a marina. Find these at Channel Marker 60 in the Intracoastal Waterway, north of Captiva; accessible only be boat.

◆
CAPE CORAL

A relaxing place to stay and enjoy the outdoor life with 14 recreational parks. There are fishing opportunities in **Four**

Freedoms Park and several others, as well as playgrounds and picnic facilities. Ecology Park features a nature trail and observation tower and **Lake Kennedy** has a beach. Cape Coral is a mainland coastal community bordering the Intracoastal Waterway, looking across to Pine Island.

CAPTIVA ISLAND

It was to this tiny island that pirate José Gaspar, who plundered his way through the islands which are now Lee County, sent his captives. This is a Florida version of Tahiti: lush, encircled by white sand and mangroves, and colorful with hibiscus.

There are two major resorts. At **South Seas Plantation**, guests can opt for a hotel room, villa or guest cottage; choose from several places to dine; play golf or tennis, or take sailing lessons at the marina, or join a fishing or shelling charter.

Shelling is the main attraction on Captiva. Simply walk along **Blind Pass Beach** and you can see loads of them spilled on to the shore with each fresh wave. Miniscule but colorful coquinas are the most common; you might find a sand dollar (a bleached white circle) or the rare black shark's teeth.

Other activities include watersports and biking. Surprisingly there are nearly a dozen restaurants on Captiva. Six miles (9.6km) long, this is a sister island to Sanibel, to which it is connected. An extensive wetland tract with nature trails lies between the two islands, which are easily reached from the mainland via a 1-mile (1.6km) toll causeway.

◆
CAYO COSTA

Cayo Costa is the region's largest undeveloped barrier island, only purchased by the state in 1985, and only accessible by boat. It is being developed into a state park – the Florida Department of Natural Resources maintains primitive cabins in the northern section, near Johnson Shoals – but most visitors come for the day to fish, swim, hunt for shells or venture inland to admire the native flora. Many shorebirds nest here in spring and in summer, and sea turtles lay their eggs on the beaches.

◆
ESTERO ISLAND

One of the most popular and lively destinations in the area, this is the site of Fort Myers Beach. Because there are no bad undertows or dangerous riptides, this is a particularly safe beach for children. Compared with some of the other islands, Estero's social life is quite racy. All the hotels are by the beach; all the restaurants serve fresh seafood, including red snapper and grouper. You could even catch your own – from the numerous piers and docks, or by joining a charter boat from one of the marinas in search of tarpon. Watersports include jet skis, catamarans and parasailing.

Family amusements include unusual golf courses: **Jungle Golf**, a miniature course surrounded by larger-than-life African animals; or **Smugglers Cove** links, set amid pirates and shipwrecks (both on the San Carlos Road).

◆◆◆
FORT MYERS

This city is the hub of activity for the region, with shopping malls, restaurants and nightclubs. Thomas Alva Edison predicted that Fort Myers would become a popular metropolis when he built a winter home here in the 1880s. Today, his 14-acre estate has become the **Edison Museum**.

The tropical gardens are a major feature; Edison planted flowers and trees here for experimental purposes. He studied species like hibiscus, Rose of China, Moreton Bay figs

Phonograph horns in the Edison Museum form an unusual bouquet

and vine trees; in the hope of yielding some beneficial product. His experiments with golden rod on the estate actually did produce a new strain of plants which grew to 14ft (4m) and were 12 percent rubber! Edison also started planting McGregor Boulevard (which passes the home) with stately royal palms. The city took over the project in 1917, and the Avenue of Palms now stretches for 15 miles (24km). Edison's first view of Fort Myers was on a trip down the Caloosahatchee River. Certainly the climate influenced his decision to stay, but he also had his eye on the wild bamboo growing along the river banks, as he was using bamboo filaments in his new electric lights.

The house you see today is still lit by light bulbs Edison made in 1912. But the electric light was only one of over 1,000 inventions which he patented. The old laboratory where he worked is open to the public for guided tours, as is the museum (added since Edison's time), containing the most complete collection of his inventions, as well as personal mementoes.

Adjacent is the winter home of Edison's close friend, Henry Ford, which can be visited on a guided tour. It features 1920s period furnishings and there are plans for a museum. **Fort Myers Historical Museum** is a Spanish-style depot with displays on the Caloosas, cowmen and the Koreshans. The latter were a religious group who advocated the strange combination of celibacy and world domination. They moved from Chicago to Estero Island in the 1890s in the hope of founding a New Jerusalem. Their home is now a State Historic Area. The museum also houses a scale model of Fort Myers at the turn of the century, a large glass collection and an early transportation display.

Visitors can take a self-guided tour around the restored hub of Fort Myers, which runs along First Street, with its old style shopping arcades and restaurants – maps are available from the downtown tourist center. Fort Myers is closed on Saturdays.

Musicals, concerts and dance performances are frequently staged at the **Barbara B Mann Performing Arts Hall** on the campus of Edison Community College, adjoining a Gallery of Fine Art.

Star shows are given at the new planetarium at the **Nature Center of Lee County** on Ortiz Avenue. Children may enjoy the lights, water and music display at **Waltzing Waters** in San Carlos Park. The Everglades Jungle Cruise, from Fort Myers Yacht Basin, offers a choice of tropical island buffet, night time dinner cruise or excursions to Lake Okeechobee.

In North Fort Myers, **The Shell Factory** is a good place for buying gifts and souvenirs; shells, corals and other merchandise is spread over 70,000 square feet (6,500sq m) of space.

GASPARILLA ISLAND
This was the island where pirate José Gaspar buried his booty. Today **Boca Grande** has become a haven for the rich and famous. It was founded by the DuPont family in the late 1800s and can now offer waterside accommodations, charming shops and restaurants. Visitors may amble on the beach here, admire the old lighthouse or cycle down shady Banyan Street. Most of all they come to fish, especially for the thrill of hooking tarpon. This is the Lee Island Coast's northernmost island.

PINE ISLAND
Situated next to Gasparilla and parallel to Captiva, North Captiva and Cayo Costa islands, this island is named for its towering pines, and is accessible by bridge. Facing the Sound, it has always been known in the past for commercial fishing, and as yet it has no high rise hotels or tourist attractions but wildlife tours of the island are available. The small waterfront village of Bokeelia is a remnant of an older Florida, with nearby marinas you can set off to pay a visit to the more remote islands.

SANIBEL ISLAND
Along with her sister isle, Captiva, Sanibel is the easiest to reach and the most popular, with a happy balance between nature and modern development. The main thoroughfare is Periwinkle Way, a pretty road canopied by Australian pines. From the Sanibel Lighthouse, on the island's eastern tip, to Tarpon Bay Road, it is dotted with craft shops, boutiques and cosy restaurants. Works of the area's most successful artists can be purchased at **The Schoolhouse** and **Matsumoto Galleries**.
Visitors can stay in resort hotels, play golf and tennis here, and bicycling includes

Luxurious properties have not spoiled the beauty of Sanibel Island

children's motorcross, tandems and fringed surreys; but the most popular activity is shelling – an obsession in Sanibel. Everyone here seems to be afflicted with the "Sanibel stoop" in their search for tiger's eyes, kitten paws, angel wings and ladies' ears. If they can't be found on the beach, they can be bought in one of the innumerable shell stores, but here it is difficult to avoid buying shells which have been "taken alive" (see **Peace and Quiet**, page 108). This island's configuration makes it one of the world's three best shelling beaches, since the smooth and gentle slope of the gulf bottom allows even the most fragile shells to be brought in undamaged.

In the northern half of the island is the **J N "Ding" Darling National Wildlife Refuge**, which can be visited by bicycle or car. From the 5-mile (8km) roadway built on top of a dyke it is easy to spot heron, egrets, plovers and the ibis stalking the mud flats below. There are also walking and canoe trails and osprey and brown and white pelicans can be spotted.

USEPPA ISLAND
Wealthy boaters and fishermen belong to the Useppa Island Club, but visitors can see the island (accessible only by boat) once only if they make a reservation to do so. The club is a restored version of the original mansion which millionaire Barron G Collier built in the early 1900s.

Collier's original pink promenade still exists, leading from the island's north end to the inn.

Pirate José Gaspar was one of the first to discover Useppa, which he inhabited from time to time, though his main headquarters were at Sanibel.

Accommodations
Visitors can stay at the new **Sonesta Sanibel Harbour Resort and Spa** (tel: (813) 466 4000). On Sanibel, recommendations include the **Sanibel Beach Club**, (tel: (813) 472 3382); **Ramada Inn Beach & Tennis Resort** (tel: (813) 472 4123); **Sanibel Island Hilton Inn** (tel: (813) 472 3181); **Shell Island Beach Club** (tel: (813) 472 4497); and **Signal Inn Beach & Racquetball Club**. At Fort Myers Beach is the **Outrigger Beach Resort** (tel: (813) 463 3131). There are many reasonably priced motels here and in Fort Myers itself.

Children
The islands are fine for the very young who are happy with paddling and sand castles, but there are not many special activities. The best place for family attractions is North Fort Myers.

Restaurants
Fresh fish is the ideal order at local restaurants on the larger islands such as Estero, but Fort Myers has the widest choice.

Shopping
The biggest choice of stores is in Fort Myers and Fort Myers Beach.

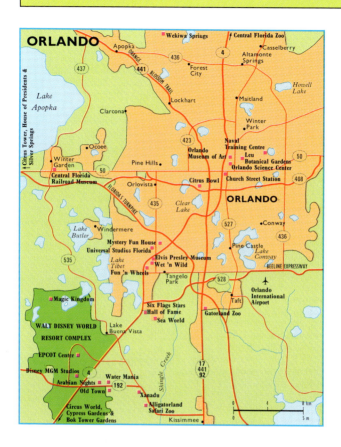

ORLANDO

Wekiwa Springs
Central Florida Zoo
Casselberry
Apopka
ORANGE
438
4
Altamonte Springs
437
441
Forest City
BLOSSOM TRAIL
Howell Lake
Citrus Tower, House of Presidents & Silver Springs
Lake Apopka
Lockhart
Maitland
Clarcona
Winter Park
423
Ocoee
Naval Training Centre
Orlando Museum of Art
Leu
Winter Garden
Pine Hills
Botanical Gardens
50
50
Orlando Science Center
Central Florida Railroad Museum
Orlovista
Citrus Bowl
Church Street Station
408
FLORIDA'S TURNPIKE
435
Clear Lake
ORLANDO
527
Conway
Lake Butler
Windermere
436
Mystery Fun House
Pine Castle
Universal Studios Florida
Lake Conway
535
Elvis Presley Museum
Lake Tibet
Wet 'n Wild
BEELINE EXPRESSWAY
Fun 'n Wheels
Tangelo Park
528
Orlando International Airport
Magic Kingdom
Taft
Six Flags Stars
Hall of Fame
Gatorland Zoo
WALT DISNEY WORLD
Lake Buena Vista
Sea World
RESORT COMPLEX
EPCOT Center
Shingle Creek
Disney MGM Studios
4
Water Mania
17 441 92
Arabian Nights
192
Old Town
Xanadu
Circus World, Cypress Gardens & Bok Tower Gardens
Alligatorland Safari Zoo
Kissimmee
0   4   8 km
0   5 m

ORLANDO & VICINITY

Think of the center of Florida – the Orlando area – and one feature is likely to spring to mind: theme parks. A host of these parks are scattered in and around a city which in the past 50 or so years has grown from a small trading post on a cattle range into an impressive, landscaped modern city with its own much-admired international airport. This middle state region occupies the spread between Ocala National Forest and Lake Okeechobee. Originally cattle country, it became better known for its citrus orchards in the 1800s, once farmers learned how profitable they could be. Today's visitors will find both rodeos and orange groves, not to mention horse farms.

Although most tourists come here for the human-made

attractions, Orlando and vicinity boast innumerable natural attributes. Central Florida is not called "Lake Country" for nothing; there are literally thousands of lakes, and two of the state's largest rivers, the Peace and Kissimmee, flow through here. There may not be a coastline or lovely beaches, but there are limitless opportunities for watersports.

Some of the fun and fantasy parks predate World War II, but it was Disney's decision to purchase a site in the mid 1960s that sparked the development whose results can be seen today.

Hotels and motels mushroomed; transportation facilities were vastly improved; hundreds of restaurants opened; small towns became vacation centers. Orlando itself is not the only holiday base; Kissimmee/St Cloud, for example, is a resort area in its own right within equal proximity to major places of interest, as well as to the airport.

WHAT TO SEE IN AND AROUND ORLANDO

◆
ALLIGATORLAND SAFARI ZOO
4580 West Irlo Bronson Memorial Highway, Kissimmee/St Cloud.
A chance to see Florida's wildlife along a mile-long (1.6km) trail. There are over 2,000 alligators in the park, ranging from babies to 1,500 pounders!

◆
APOPKA
A useful base for **Wekiwa Springs State Park** where you can camp, picnic, swim or rent a canoe. The town is in central Florida, 8 miles (13km) northwest of Orlando.

◆◆
ARABIAN NIGHTS
Kissimmee.
This attraction was developed at a cost of $20 million. The stadium, designed as an Arabian palace, can seat 1,000 and visitors dine while watching a 20-act show. The entertainment features talented horses and includes famous Lippizzanas, Quarter Horses and American Saddlebreds. They also recreate Ben Hur's chariot race. East of the intersection of Interstate 4 with Highway 192.

◆
CENTRAL FLORIDA RAILROAD MUSEUM
Winter Garden.
What used to be the Tavares & Gulf Railroad Depot, built in 1913, has been restored to exact detail. There are some 3,000 pieces of railway history on display here including many antiques and steam engines. Admission is free. A 15-minute drive from Orlando, off US50.

◆
CENTRAL FLORIDA ZOO
Sanford.
This 110-acre park has nature trails meandering through Florida woodlands and a petting corner with pony rides keeps the smaller ones happy. Take Interstate 4 (exit 52).

The Orlando area is a playground for people of all ages

◆
CLERMONT

A possible vacation base in central Florida, in the heart of citrus country that is close to many of the region's theme parks. It is most notable for its 200ft (60m) high **Citrus Tower**, from which you can see millions of citrus trees. Take the Citrus Grove Tram, Tour through a 10-acre (4-hectare) grove. On North Highway in Clermont is the **House of Presidents** where life-like wax figures of past US leaders, to President Reagan, are on display.

◆◆◆
CYPRESS GARDENS

near Winter Haven.
One of Florida's showplaces, which can truly claim to appeal to all the family. The park covers 223 acres these days, though when it started in the 1930s it comprised only 16 acres and its main attraction was the exotic botanical gardens. There are still 16 acres of flower-lined pathways with more than 8,000 varieties of plants from 75 different countries on display at various times of the year. One highlight is the 1,500-year-old giant bald cypress tree, representing the native plants which gave the gardens their name. Another special feature is the annual chrysanthemum festival in November when as many as two million of these flowers are in bloom. It's colorful any time of year,

though, and visitors may enjoy it by guided tour, by taking a leisurely walk or by electric boat ride.

In the **Animal Forest** zoological park there is plenty to see: an Exotic Bird Revue, a daily alligator handling demonstration, an oceanic and wading bird exhibit, a walk-through aviary and a special corner where young animals may be petted. Young and old alike seem to like this particular area with its pygmy goats, baby camels and huge Aldabra tortoises, and they are also able to view a two-level prairie dog habitat.

The main attraction of **Southern Crossroads**, a replica *antebellum* town, is a much-photographed southern mansion, but this section of the park also features shops, restaurants, street performers and bands. The Island in the

Sky ride is a great observation point; nearby fountains and statues make good backdrops for photographs, and Whistlestop USA houses an elaborate railway exhibit. Undoubtedly, Cypress Gardens is best known for its skillful and exciting waterski shows, but there is also a water spectacular where high-dive record holders perform outstanding feats, and displays are given of synchronized swimming and snowski aerial acrobatics. Another show (the only permanent themed ice show in the southeastern US) features the talents of the finest professional skaters in a Broadway style revue. Under 3's are admitted free; otherwise the one admission price covers everything. Well worth a day's visit. Located off US27.

◆◆◆
DISNEY WORLD
Undoubtedly Florida's number one attraction, covering a staggering 27,443 acres (11,100 hectares)! One of the newer attractions is the **Disney-MGM Studios Theme Park**, a growing section with its own visitor center, shows and themed lands, based upon such movies as *Star Wars* and *Honey, I Shrunk the Kids*. Visitors can tour the backstage production facilities and there is a "Great Movie Rail" through classic film sets, a recreated 1930s Hollywood Boulevard, and a replica of Mann's Chinese Theatre. Another new feature is the **Pleasure Island** – an

island entertainment complex linked by footbridge from Disney World Village. It has restaurants, shops selling a variety of merchandise, a 10-screen theater and street entertainment, but its main attractions are its six nightclubs. At Mannequins, the emphasis is on clever dance floor staging and lighting, and mannequins (live and animated) mingle with the crowd; Neon Armadillo Music Saloon features country music, its focal point a tall artificial cactus supporting a neon armadillo! Both of these are for over 21s, but children accompanied by an adult may enter The Comedy Warehouse, with its improvisational comedy troupe, and the Adventurers Club, modeled on the private clubs of bygone days. Here each room has a theme and animation and special effects are used in true Disney fashion. The Mask Room, for example, is decorated with animated masks – among them "Comedia" and "Tragedia" – who converse with themselves and guests.
More of Disney's special effects are to be seen in the Club Library and the main salon where the Nauga (an animated Disney creation) introduces visitors to some of the other animated attractions. The Zephyr Rockin' Roller Dome is meant for all the family. This is a three-tiered structure combining food, music and roller skating. Both the band music and the dress of the waiting staff are straight

Disney World, opened in 1971, covers over 27,000 acres, rivaling California's Disneyland

out of the '50s. Perhaps the most dramatic feature is the disc jockey, who works in an electronic capsule suspended by crane, so that he is able to move freely about all three of the club's levels.

Videopolis is a nightclub primarily for those between 12 and 21. Naturally there are videos, dramatic lighting and a stainless steel floor for dancing. Nonalcoholic special drinks are a unique feature and in the studios next to the club guests can create and play their own videos and recording tapes.

Novelty shops line Chandlery Row; dining options include the Portobello Yacht Club (an upscale restaurant with northern Italian specialities) and the Fireworks Factory (more casual, serving barbecued ribs and chicken).

ORLANDO

There is no extra charge for Pleasure Island during the day; at night, one fee covers all entertainments (over 18s only). The World's **Magic Kingdom** is still a favorite, its "lands" continuing to attract millions of visitors. Through the turnstiles you enter Main Street, where there are gift shops and vintage vehicles to ride, including a horse-drawn trolley. This leads to Town Square, a good spot for lunch. The Kingdom's famous landmark, Cinderella Castle, is a part of Fantasyland, the area most popular with small children where live Disney musicals take place. It's a Small World – where colorful singing and dancing dolls represent children from around the world – is a must, as is 20,000 Leagues Under the Sea, a ride which gives the illusion of being in a submarine.

In Adventureland, you can take the Pirates of the Caribbean ride past fantastic audio-

Cinderella Castle towers over Fantasyland, a favorite for small children in Disney's Magic Kingdom

animatronic sets; and enjoy the Jungle Cruise, one of the Disney masterpieces. Frontierland recreates frontier days. The big thrill ride here is Big Thunder Mountain; the very young enjoy Country Bear Jamboree; and pent-up energy can be spent on Tom Sawyer Island.

Liberty Square is another good place to eat (no alcoholic drinks are served in The Magic Kingdom's restaurants), to watch the particularly lifelike presentation of the Hall of Presidents, or to pay a visit to the Haunted Mansion.

A "people-mover" takes you alongside or through most of Tomorrowland's attractions; or you could reach this area by aerial tramway. Still a popular ride here is Space Mountain, where capsule "rockets" hurtle down a dark cone aided by special effects – the under 3's are not allowed on this ride. Dreamflight explores aviation history, including hypersonic flight. There is also Mickey's Starland, created to honor the world's most famous mouse when he turned 60.

Part of Disneyworld, but a separate entity with its own entrance charge is **EPCOT**. Its newest pavilion is Norway, where guests ride Viking boats on a mysterious Nordic voyage, sample typical Scandinavian fare or browse through the Norwegian shops. It is one of 11 countries' showcases. The UK pavilion features a pub (alcohol is allowed at EPCOT); or you could eat at the first class restaurant in the French pavilion, or watch the Japanese dancers. Mexico's pyramid is among the most atmospheric, with smouldering volcano effects and the strolling *mariachis*, and the street bazaars of the Morocco pavilion are naturally colorful. World Showcase is only one part of the EPCOT center, however. The other half is called Future World, where the silvery landmark is Spaceship Earth, a time machine in which you ride from the past to the stars. All the Future World pavilions are sponsored by large companies such as Kodak and AT & T and provide education in a fascinating way, using hands-on exhibits and special effects. The 3-D movie *Captain EO*, Michael Jackson's space age adventure, can be seen in Journey into Imagination; Horizons gives you a glimpse of life in the future; tomorrow's transportation is portrayed in World of Motion. Day and multiple-day tickets for the Magic Kingdom cover all the attractions, the same applies at EPCOT and combination passes are also available.

There is still more to see at Disney World (for which there is a separate charge). **Fort Wilderness** is a wooded site for campers, and an area which offers a variety of sports including trail rides, canoe rental and nature trails. Near the resort, **Discovery Island** is a tropical oasis with a change of pace from the rest of the Disney property, a sanctuary for African cranes, peacocks and scarlet ibis.

River Country has a heated outdoor pool, and a number of devices shoot swimmers from air to water, including flumes and slides.

Boating at The World could mean a trip on Bay Lake or Seven Seas Lagoon.

The newest water entertainment area is Typhoon Lagoon where swimmers can snorkel amid tropical fish, plummet down streams of a volcanic mountain or ride the waves in a large inland surfing lagoon.

There are many rental options, from speedboats to canoes or canopied pontoons. Golfers have their choice of several championship courses, and there's a miniature course for beginners.

Shops, restaurants and accommodations are to be found throughout Disney World. The Grand Floridian Beach Resort Hotel by the Seven Seas Lagoon, is a resort in itself. The new family-priced Caribbean Beach Resort, made up of "villages" designed in Caribbean styles, provides more than 2,000 rooms.

ELVIS PRESLEY MUSEUM
6544 Carrier Dr, Orlando.
Dedicated to the late rock singer, this museum displays some 250 items associated with Presley, from Graceland guitars and personal accessories to cars and clothing used in his films. Under 6's admitted free.

FUN 'N' WHEELS
International Drive, Orlando.
You don't have to pay to sample the rides in this 4-acre park.

Recommended if you have smaller children in tow – there are go-karts, water slides, bumper cars and boats, a ferris wheel and an 18-hole mini golf course.

GATORLAND ZOO
Yes, this does mean alligators, and there are 5,000 of them! The zoo is a commercial alligator farm and research facility, as well as being a tourist attraction. If you've always wanted to hold an alligator, this is the place to visit; and don't worry – they're either nonbiting babies or carefully muzzled. You could also take one of the nature trails through a cypress swamp for a close look at Florida wildlife.

This zoo was the setting for some of the film *Indiana Jones and the Temple of Doom*. Located between Orlando and Kissimmee; take US441 and follow the signs.

HARRY P LEU GARDENS
Lake Rowena, N Orlando.
These relaxing gardens feature all kinds of exotic plants; the rose garden and orchid house are of particular interest. Leu House, a turn-of-the-century farmhouse, has been restored as a museum reflecting the lifestyle of the period.
Take US441.

KISSIMMEE/ST CLOUD
An ideal vacation base only a 25-minute drive from Orlando's international airport and within easy reach of many theme

Alligators can be held or seen at a safe distance in Gatorland Zoo

parks. It was first settled in 1878; in 1880 Broadway, now one of its main avenues, was still covered in Bermuda grass, had boardwalks on either side and a railroad down the center. Today the area attracts thousands of visitors. It is Tupperware's world headquarters (no admission charge to tour through) and has an unusual monument on Monument Avenue (downtown), built with stones from every state in the country. One of its own main features is **Old Town**, a speciality turn-of-the-century shopping and eating area patterned after a turn-of-the-century Florida town, where you can visit a wood-carving museum, ride an antique carousel or take a horse-drawn surrey.

Also in town is Xanadu, a home of the future portraying life in the 21st century. Not to be missed is Medieval Life (next to Medieval Times) where visitors can experience life as it was 1,000 years ago. Authentically dressed inhabitants give various demonstrations including birds of prey in flight and hunting dogs at work.

The city is in central Florida.

◆
LAKE WALES
Away from the usual hustle and bustle, this resort, which is situated on Lake Kissimmee, supplies all the lakeside recreation you could wish for; with fishing, boating and nature

trails. But it is best known for **Bok Tower Gardens** at the top of Iron Mountain, a peaceful retreat built in the early 1900s by Dutch immigrant Edward Bok. The 225-foot (78m) tower houses a 57-bell carillon which gives daily recitals at 3:00P.M..

◆
MYSTERY FUN HOUSE
Major Boulevard, Orlando.
This amusement complex has surprises galore in 15 chambers, including an Indiana Jones-style walk through adventure, and a miniature golf course.

◆◆
ORLANDO
A vibrant hub of central Florida, this is a city whose name still gives rise to debate. Some say it was named in honor of Shakespeare's hero in *As You Like It*; others claim the name was chosen to commemorate Orlando Reeves, a messenger, who was killed by Indians on the site.

52

ORLANDO

Today Orlando is a popular base for a variety of theme parks and attractions and has many of its own, especially on International Drive. Universal Studios Florida, which opened in 1990, is a growing entertaining enterprise where visitors may watch actual filming and succumb to special effects.
Orlando also boasts its own Science Center and is the focal point for many festivals. There are almost 50 city parks and over 50 lakes within the city limits. A variety of architectural styles can be seen, like the National Bank Building (1929), the Kress Building or the art deco McCrory's Five and Dime (1906). And you could make a Friday stop at the Orlando Naval Training Center when a 50-state salute is given at graduation ceremonies at 9:45A.M..

REPTILE WORLD SERPENTARIUM
St Cloud.
This Serpentarium was originally founded as a research center for the production and distribution of snake venoms. Now, however, it encourages visitors to learn more about reptiles and take a close-up, but safe view of cobras, pythons and rattlesnakes. Located 4 miles (6km) east of St Cloud on Highway 192 (closed Mondays and September).

SEA WORLD
7007 Sea World Drive, Orlando.
This is an ideal place for families: the various antics, shows and exhibits always delight the children. Killer whales, dolphins, sea lions and otters are all stars in their own pools. There are feeding demonstrations, Japanese pearl

Killer whales are star performers in Sea World's displays

diving exhibitions, a Shark Encounter and Penguin Exhibition as well as waterski shows.

◆
SILVER SPRINGS
Ocala.
A natural wonder whose springs discharge 500 million gallons of water each day. On the recreational side, visitors may take a jeep safari jungle cruise or glass-bottom boat ride, inspect a collection of vintage cars or prehistoric canoes and visit the deer park or the fascinating reptile institute.

◆
WATER MANIA
West Highway 192, Kissimmee.
One way to keep cool on a hot day! Water Mania features a wave pool and several thrilling water slides. The park covers 24 acres (10 hectares) and also includes an activity area for children, a pleasant sandy beach and picnic spot.

◆◆
WET 'N' WILD
International Drive, Orlando.
This water park, only a 10-minute ride from Disney World, has huge water slides and a wave pool. There are thrills on the six-story high Der Stuka; relaxation on the Lazy River; fun at the latest attraction – The Black Hole.

Accommodations
You are spoiled for choice here. The number of motels, hotels, resorts and short-term rental units available increases each year. If Walt Disney World is your top priority and you do

Going for a swim takes nerves of steel at the Wet 'n' Wild water park

not have a rental car, accommodations on Disney land, offering complimentary transportation to and from The World's sights, are your best bet. The enormous Contemporary Resort with its atrium lobby, through which the monorail travels, is closest to The Magic Kingdom; and the Hilton at Walt Disney World Village, Lake Buena Vista, is closest to EPCOT (see **What to see**, above), but there are many others within the complex and several just outside, such as the fashionable Cypress Hyatt Regency, which also has courtesy transportation. Disney World Resort Hotels include:
Disney Inn, located bear Palm and Magnolia championship golf courses. In addition to

54

ORLANDO

luxury accommodations, there
are putting greens, driving
ranges, lighted tennis courts
plus a swimming pool. Country
club atmosphere but suited to
families.

Contemporary Resort, situated
on Bay Lake adjacent to the
Magic Kingdom, this 15-story
A-frame tower hotel, with north
and south accommodation
wings, is the most popular. The
Magic Kingdom monorail
arrives in its lobby and there's a
good view from its Top of the
World supper club.

Polynesian Village Resort, in
the Polynesian Village section of
The World conveys a South
Seas atmosphere. Guest rooms
are located in "long houses";
the swimming pool has its own
waterfall and is surrounded by
tropical foliage; *luau*
(Polynesian feasts) are given
nightly.

Grand Floridian Resort, 900-
room luxury, turn-of-the-
century style hotel next to
Seven Seas Lagoon.

Caribbean Beach Resort, is
one of the newer hotels,
southeast of EPCOT Center,
with over 2,000 rooms, six
restaurants and seven pools. In
1990, the architecturally striking
Walt Disney World Dolphin
and **Walt Disney World Swan**
also joined the complex of on-
site hotels. On and around
Highway 192, there is even
more choice. Park Inn
International, an all suite hotel;
Ramada Resort Maingate East at
the Parkway; Howard Johnson
Fountain Park Plaza; and Wilson
World Hotel are all in the
Kissimmee St Cloud area. There
are many budget motels, too.

Children
This part of Florida couldn't be
better, with amusements for
all ages. Wax museums,
alligator zoos, thrilling water
rides, medieval jousting,
dolphin shows and waterski
revues are just some of the
temptations.

Restaurants
There is a multitude of
restaurants to suit all pockets
and tastes, from fast food to
gourmet spreads. A variety of
eating places exists at most of
the theme parks. At Disney
World options include a
Polynesian *luau*, dinner on a
riverboat, or a fried chicken
and ribs dinner show; and at
EPCOT many of the national
pavilions feature regional food.
A favorite Orlando complex is
Church Street Station, which
offers several themed eating
areas with entertainment.
Orlando's newest set meal
possibility is **Sleuths**, a
mystery dinner theater that
serves up intrigue to go with
your food.
Fort Liberty in Kissimmee
features a Western banquet
and entertainment in a
stockade fort setting. Other
unusual set meal possibilities
include **Medieval Times** in
Kissimmee and **King Henry's
Feast** in Orlando.

Shopping
Interesting gift shops are to be
found at all the theme park
attractions, in the heart of
Orlando, such as at the Church
Street Station Exchange or the
Mercado Mediterranean
Village, and in Kissimmee's
Old Town.

"St Pete" Beach, a resort connected to the mainland by causeway

THE PINELLAS

When Spanish explorers sailed around Florida's west coast in the early 1500's they saw an area which they called *punta pinal*, or "point of pines." From that name comes today's word Pinellas, which refers to a string of eight resort communities along 128 miles (206km) of white sand.

Altogether, this "suncoast playground" takes up 265 square miles (680sq km) from Tarpon Springs in the north to St Petersburg in the south. The "suncoast" title is promotional – but records maintain that the area enjoys an average of 361 days of sunshine a year.

As a resort destination for Americans, The Pinellas are not new. This leisure discovery was made years ago, once Henry Plant had extended his railroad and steamship routes into Tampa in the 1880s and opened the glamorous Tampa Bay Hotel in 1891. Nowadays, Tampa is an international gateway served by many airlines including USAir, Delta and TWA, and accommodations range from the sleek and sophisticated to the more affordable seaside motels.

The Pinellas tends to be less expensive than the more familiar eastern "Gold Coast" (Miami and the Palm Beaches), yet it is just as near the attractions of Orlando (Disney World, etc) and boasts some of its own. The region has evolved into a casual, relaxed and reasonably priced part of

THE PINELLAS

Florida.

Watersports are available here all year round – from simple swimming to the more invigorating jet skiing and parasailing. The area is well noted for fishing, particularly off shore, deep sea; the tarpon appear in late spring/early summer. Some of the resort properties specialize in tennis or golf, with beautiful court locations and scenic courses. For those who would rather watch than participate, there is also football, baseball, dog racing and jai alai (a game related to pelota).

The emphasis in The Pinellas is on relaxation, but there is a lively cultural life here, too, with orchestral productions, ballet and arts festivals. St Petersburg's Bayfront Center and Clearwater's Richard Baumgardner Center for the Performing Arts both offer a particularly wide range of activities. Some of the communities here have a European air – Dunedin, for example, where the Scots settled in 1870 and still celebrate the Highland Games in April; or the Greek Tarpon Springs. In addition to the mainland resort, there are the two islands of Honeymoon and Caladesi (see **What to see**).

WHAT TO SEE IN AND AROUND THE PINELLAS

CALADESI ISLAND
The name is Spanish for "beautiful bayou," and this state park may only be reached by boat (private or ferry service

Ivory sands at Clearwater Beach, part of the city of Clearwater

from Clearwater, Clearwater Beach and nearby Honeymoon Island). Yucca and palms add their own grace to this peaceful isle, which covers 1,400 acres, three miles (5km) off shore from Dunedin Beach. It is a refuge for wading birds, but there are food and picnic facilities, a children's playground and 2 miles (3km) of white sand.

This is an ideal place for swimming, shelling or fishing, skin and scuba diving and nature study – a three-mile (5km) trail winds through the interior. For a view of the whole island, there is a 60ft (18m) observation tower.

♦♦♦
CLEARWATER

Visitors here will soon
understand Clearwater's
nickname – "The Sparkling
City." The Gulf waters do
sparkle in the sun, and
watersports are given high
priority. This is the seat of
Pinellas County, both a growing
city community and a coastal
community with a 2-mile (3km)
expanse of white sandy beach.
This ivory beach is one of the
most popular, and Clearwater
itself is perhaps the most
fashionable community. Here
you can fish from **Pier 60**,
which stretches out into the
Gulf, rent a boat from the
marina or take a cruise. Several
are available, including picnic
cruises on a pirate ship, and

one which offers on-board
dinner dances. Events include
the Kahlua Cup International
Yacht races in November.
The **Marine Science Center**,
a research facility on Windward
Passage, displays marine life
(live and model), including
baby sea turtles and dolphins
(eight to 16-year-olds can
attend marine biology class
here in summer. Classes free;
but there is a charge to enter).
Ruth Eckerd Hall on
McMullen-Booth Road is part of
the performing arts complex,
presenting not only music but
dance, fun and fantasy, with
regular art exhibitions in its
gallery. The Florida Orchestra
is based here and the Florida
Opera gives performances
during the year.
Next to the St Petersburg-
Clearwater airport,
Yesterday's Air Force
features restored aircraft and
aviation artifacts dating from
World War II. Nearby
Boatyard Village is a recreated late 19th-century
fishing village, with shops,
restaurants and a theater. By
way of contrast to the human-
made, take a look at **Moccasin
Lake Nature Park**, east of
US19, where most of the area's
native plant and animal species
are to be found. A 1-mile
(1.6km) nature trail winds
through the 50-acre park and
there are wildlife exhibits and
displays at the Interpretive
Center.

♦
DUNEDIN

This resort, which adjoins
Clearwater, was founded by

Scots in 1870 and their influence is evident in the architecture, the street names and, of course, the festivities. In fact, the settlement used to be known as Jonesboro, until two enterprising merchants petitioned the government for a post office to increase business for their store. They requested the name "Dunedin," a Gaelic term meaning "peaceful rest." Peaceful it is, except perhaps during the Highland Games in April, when the bagpipes come out along with dancing and drumming, and booths selling Scottish wares and food.
Before the railway, Dunedin was one of the chief ports between Cedar Key and Key West for the shipping of fruit and vegetables. A visit is recommended to the **Railroad Historical Museum** on Main Street, which was a station for the Orange Belt Railroad system dating from 1889. Drawings and relics from the Scottish community's past are displayed here (closed June to September). Among other registered buildings are Andrews Memorial Chapel and J O Douglas House. There is no admission fee to see the **Fine Arts and Cultural Center** on Michigan Avenue, with its gallery featuring some impressive exhibits and an arts and crafts shop.

HOLIDAY ISLES
This is the collective name given to several beaches in The Pinellas: Indian Shores, Indian Rocks Beach, Belleair Beach, Redington Shores, North Redington Shores and Redington Beach. Novice sailors may rent boats from any of these beaches, which offer 10 miles (16km) of sand and Florida's longest fishing pier, at Indian Rocks.
Indian Rocks Beach is the site of **Hamlin's Landing**, a Victorian waterfront shopping and dining complex alongside the Intracoastal Waterway. Two exceptional Pinella attractions are also to be found at Indian Shores. The **Suncoast Seabird Sanctuary** is Dr Ralph Heath's hospital for birds on an acre plot near the beach on Gulf Boulevard. Dr Heath was 25 when he saw a cormorant struggling with a broken wing in the middle of a highway. He rescued the bird and treated it, the news spread, and soon other sufferers were arriving. What was once a temporary casualty department has become permanent with its own operating theater and intensive care unit. Over 40 species reside here, including the largest collection of brown pelicans in captivity. Injured birds, it seems, frequently find their way to this sanctuary, and those that recover enough to fly again are released. Dr Heath is usually on hand to answer questions from visitors. Among the stories he tells is one of a pelican with a broken wing which dragged itself for a mile (1.6km) to reach the sanctuary gate; and another of two crippled pelicans who produced the first offspring to be hatched and raised in

captivity. There is no entrance charge here, but donations are happily accepted since it is a nonprofit making organization – and visitors are encouraged to adopt a bird. **Tiki Gardens** also on Gulf Boulevard has a South Seas atmosphere in its 13-acre tropical exhibit: flowers, birds, plants and monkeys can be seen along The Polynesian Adventure Trail. Additionally, there are shops selling merchandise from around the world and a restaurant specializing in Polynesian food.

HONEYMOON ISLAND
Like neighboring Caladesi Island, this is one of the few undisturbed barrier islands in the Gulf of Mexico, but Honeymoon does have access to the mainland via the Dunedin Causeway. Now a state park, it provides for outdoor activities such as swimming, shelling, fishing, picnics and nature study.

LARGO
There are two reasons for a visit here. The **Heritage Park & Museum** on 125th Street North comprises a fascinating collection of restored homes and buildings in a pine wood setting. The actual museum forms the centerpiece, holding examples of pioneer life at the turn of the century and often showing craft demonstrations. Admission free (closed Mondays).

On the same street, **Suncoast Botanical Gardens** feature a variety of cacti and local flora including eucalyptus trees sometimes as tall as 85ft (26m), palms, crepe myrtle and other plants. Admission is free.

MADEIRA BEACH

A popular resort community at the center of The Pinellas, this has one of the best fishing inlets

Tradition by design: John's Pass fishing village, Madeira Beach

60

THE PINELLAS

in the state, at John's Pass, whether for big game or easy fishing. Visitors can rent a charter boat and head for the deep seas or inland fishing on Boca Ciega Bay – or merely throw a line from the docks. **John's Pass Village & Boardwalk**, designed as a traditional fishing village, is home to a large commercial and charter fishing fleet. Boutiques, art galleries and restaurants line the waterfront.

Many events and festivals take place here during the year and a paddle-wheel riverboat offers lunch and sightseeing cruises along the Intracoastal Waterway. The beach itself, north of John's Pass, is about 2½ miles (4km) of fine sand.

SAFETY HARBOR
This place was well known to the Indians and the Spanish for its healing mineral springs. One mile (1.6km) north of the village center, **Philippe Park's** arts museum showcases local artists' work, and a history museum displays local artifacts. The park, which overlooks Tampa Bay, was named after Count Odet Philippe, one of Napoleon's surgeons who settled the site in the 1830s. He introduced the first grapefruit trees.

ST PETERSBURG
Occupying the southern tip of the peninsula, St Petersburg is the most cosmopolitan of all the Pinella communities, combining city appeal with nearby "St Pete" Beach.

Although few examples of early Spanish architecture remain, there is a great deal of the pseudo-Spanish style which became so fashionable during the Florida land boom.

John Williams from Detroit founded St Petersburg in 1876 on the site of his farm. Having given up farming he turned to town planning, engaging the assistance of exiled Russian nobleman Peter Demens. They tossed a coin to see who would choose the new town's name; Demens won and named it after his birthplace.

Good weather made this a winter retreat, especially for the elderly, but these days St Petersburg is a lively, sunny resort for all ages, often referred to as the "sailing capital of the south." Many a prestigious racing event and regatta takes place annually here and it is easy for anyone to rent a variety of boats, or take a lunch or dinner cruise on Tampa Bay. The recently renovated Pier, which extends for a half mile (0.8km) into Tampa Bay, is a major landmark. The inverted pyramid structure at the end of it contains shops, aquarium, marine exhibit, an observation deck and places to eat. There is always a beach nearby – either downtown or 30 minutes or so away, on the Gulf, but St Petersburg offers more than beaches. Athletic, cultural and other entertaining events are frequently held at the **Bayfront Center. Derby Lane**, on Gandy Boulevard, features greyhound racing between January and May (not Sunday) –

*Beaches and sailing have boosted
St Petersburg's growth as a resort*

visitors can eat at the clubhouse
overlooking the track, and a
mini TV on each tables gives
closer race scrutiny. Ballroom
dancing still takes place at the
Coliseum, on Fourth Avenue,
on its 13,000-square-foot
(1,200sq-m) maple floor.
At the **Haas Museum** on
Second Avenue, restored
homes include Lowe House

built in 1850, Grace Turner
House, an old barber shop,
blacksmith's and railroad
depot. Open afternoons,
Thursday to Sunday. At
number 335, the **Historical
Museum** features thousands
of pioneer artifacts and
pictures as well as collections
of shells, coins, dolls and
chinaware. There is no
admission fee (but donations
are welcomed) for entrance to
the **Museum of Fine Arts** on

Beach Drive North, noted for its collection of French Impressionist paintings, it also has a good collection of European, American, preColumbian and Far Eastern art. Permanent period rooms feature antiques and historical furnishings. One of the highlights here is the collection of photographs by American masters. Guided tours are available. Closed Monday. Special presentations are made between September and May in the **Planetarium** at St Petersburg Junior College Science Building. This sky theater is under a large domed ceiling with scheduled performances September to May.

Art lovers visiting St Petersburg should pay a visit to the **Salvador Dali Museum** on Third Street South – the world's largest single collection of Dali works under one roof; so large that works are rotated regularly. The collection includes 93 oils, 100 watercolors and drawings, along with nearly 1,300 graphics, sculptures and objects d'art. Closed Mondays, Easter to Christmas. Under 9's free. St Petersburg's newest attraction is **Great Explorations**, on Fourth Street South – an arts and science hands-on museum. St Petersburg can appeal to nature lovers too. At the **Boyd Hill Nature Trail** on Country Club Way South, there are six trails which lead through 216 acres of natural beauty. The wildlife is fascinating and guided tours are available.

There are signs of revival in the Tarpon Springs sponge industry

Fort DeSoto Park, accessible by the Pinellas Byway off I 275, south of St Petersburg Beach, was built during the Spanish American War and is located on Mullet Key, the largest of five islands which make up this unique country park. Fort DeSoto was built in 1898 to protect Tampa Bay, but the islands' history dates back before Ponce De Leon's arrival in the 16th century. Today, the park consists of 900 unspoiled acres with 7 miles (11km) of beaches, two fishing piers, picnic and camping area. The **Kopsick Palm Aboretum** on North Shore Drive and Tenth Avenue features a range of native palms growing in the scenic section of Northshore Park on the famous waterfront, and

Sunken Gardens on Fourth Street North, has more than 50,000 tropical plants and flowers in bloom all the year round. A walk-through aviary features tropical birds and thousands of rare orchids are in the Orchid Arbor.

St Petersburg Beach is part and parcel of St Petersburg really, yet an island resort in itself, connected to the mainland with a 7½-mile (12km) strand of beaches bordered by hotels, beach bars and restaurants. It has its own marina, charter boat fishing and sightseeing cruise boat; its own fishing jetties and sports facilities; its own discos and piano bars. **Silas' Wax Museum and Funhouse** at Silas Bayside Market (formerly the London Wax Museum) makes use of holograms and special effects to bring wax figures to life.

◆◆◆
TARPON SPRINGS

The most northerly of the Pinellas coast communities, at the point where the Anclote River widens into bayous on its way to the Gulf, Tarpon Springs was first founded in 1876. The name stems from the fact that the first settlers thought tarpon spawned in the spring's bayous, though nowadays mullet are generally to be found.

In about 1905, Greek sponge fishermen moved here from Key West, convinced that the Gulf of Mexico held rich and sizeable sponge beds which they would be able to reach now that diving equipment had improved. They were right, and more and more Greek divers followed, bringing their customs and traditions with them.

In the 1940s marine bacteria destroyed the sponges and the men took other jobs or moved away. But recently it seems that sponges have become prolific again; the problem now is persuading young people into the diving business, which involved many hours at sea. Tarpon Springs is still very Greek, however, and stores on its docks are filled with sponges in every shape and form. You might note that size does not necessarily indicate quality, and that various species are suited to various duties, from cleaning the body to cleaning the car.

Most of the activity here revolves around Dodecanese Boulevard and the **Sponge Docks**, where there are gift

1920s chic: Don Cesar's pink hotel

shops, Greek nightclubs and
tavernas. **Spongeorama** uses
diaramas and film to depict the
history of the sponge industry;
the museum is free, but there
is a charge to see the film.
Tours of the village leave from
here.
It is also worth visiting **St
Nicholas Greek Orthodox
Cathedral** on North Pinellas
Avenue, a replica of St
Sophia's in Istanbul, the focal
point of the Blessing of the
Fleet during Epiphany. George
Innes, the 19th-century
American landscape painter,
had a house and studio
overlooking Spring Bayou,
where both he and his son
worked. The largest single
collection of George Jr's work
is to be seen in the
Universalist Church, on
Read Street, Tarpon Springs.
Tarpon Springs' own Gulf
beach, Sunset, is reached after
a short drive along the
causeway.
Treasure Island
Located south of John's Pass,
Treasure Island is a Pinellas
resort with 4 miles (6km) of

white sands – indeed, some of
the broadest stretches
anywhere along the Suncoast. A
publicity stunt in the early
1900s created the name, and
the area was formed with the
merging of four communities in
1955. It still has three
subdivisions: Isle of Capri, Isle
of Palms and Paradise Island.
Watersports are an obvious
attraction: sailboats,
paddleboats and windsurf
boards may be rented from the
southern end of the island; but
there is also a golf course, and,
at the Paradise Island tennis
complex, 21 courts which are
open for public use. Pirate Day,
on 4 July, is the big celebration
here, when a mock pirate
invasion is staged to capture a
treasure chest.

Accommodations
There are hundreds of motels
with thousands of rooms in the
Pinellas as well as hotels and
condominiums. Two of the most
historic hostelries are the
Belleview Mido Resort, a

sprawling Victorian structure that was opened in the 1890s and overlooks Clearwater Harbour, and the towering "pink castle" of the **Don Cesar Beach Resort** on St Petersburg Beach, opened in the 1920s. The guest list at both has always been something of a Who's Who. The Belleview has recently undergone a multimillion dollar renovation. Also among the best are the **Sheraton Sand Key Resort** (on Clearwater Beach) with its private beach, water sports, night-lit tennis courts and entertainment Sky Lounge; and the **Breckenridge Resort Hotel** at St Petersburg Beach, whose rooms all feature kitchenettes and whose poolside bar has live entertainment. **Innisbrook Resort** at Tarpon Springs is popular with the golfing fraternity, providing 36 holes of championship golf, as well as a tennis and racquetball center and a spa and health club.

Children

The Pinellas beaches and the range of watersports are enough to keep younger members of the family happily occupied without further distractions, but the region has several other attractions for children. Busch Gardens/The Dark Continent in Tampa is only a ½ to 1 hour's drive away and is superb (see **Tampa – What to see**). Ringling's Museum with its Circus Galleries in Sarasota is easily reached, as are Orlando's popular theme parks.

Restaurants

There are well over 1,500 restaurants along this coastline, ranging from the elegant candlelit diner-for-two variety to barefoot casual, and even including moonlight dinner cruises. Seafood is a speciality and is always fresh and plentiful; try elegant **Wine Cellar** at North Redington Beach or fun place **Crabbie Bill's** at Indian Rocks Beach, or the simple but good **Friendly Fisherman** in Madeira Beach. It's worth sampling the barbecued ribs with pit-baked beans and garlic toast at the **Hickory Smoke House** in St Petersburg. There is a distinctly British touch at the **Harp and Thistle Pub** (at St Petersburg Beach), right down to the draught Guinness and Bass. For romantic dining, try the Mississippi-style sternwheeler cruise from Hamlin's Landing or dinner with entertainment at the **Showboat Dinner Theatre** in Clearwater or the **Royal Palm Dinner Theatre** in North Redington Beach; Tarpon Springs has a number of tavernas serving Greek dishes.

Shopping

The Pinellas has around 80 shopping centers and malls, though the waterfront village boutiques are the most tempting. Few can resist buying at least one sponge in Tarpon Springs. Try **Boatyard Village** in a cove on Tampa Bay for its boutiques and galleries; the speciality shops at **Hamlin's Landing** along the Intracoastal Waterway at Indian Rocks Beach; or **John's Pass Village** in Madeira Beach.

St. Nicholas Church
Spongeorama
Tarpon Springs
Universalist Church
(19)

Lake
Tarpon

Wall
Springs

Crystal Beach

Palm
Harbor

Honeymoon
Island

Ozona

(586)

Oldsmar

Caladesi
Island

(19)

Countryside

(580)

Railroad
Historical Museum
Dunedin

Moccasin Lake
Nature Park

Philippe Park

Safety
Harbor

Marine Science Center

Clearwater Beach
Pier 60

(590)

Ruth Eckerd Hall

Clearwater

(60)

COURTNEY CAMPBELL PARKWAY

Old Tampa Bay

Belleair Beach

Belleair

Boatyard
Village
St. Petersburg-Clearwater
International Airport

(686)

Yesterday's
Air Force

HOWARD

Largo

Heritage Park
& Museum
(688)

Hamlin's Landing
Suncoast
Botanical
Gardens
Indian Rocks
Beach
(595)

Pinellas

Canal

Indian Shores

Tiki Gardens

Lake
Seminole

(92)

Derby Lane

Peninsula

Cross Bayou

(699)

Suncoast
Seabird Sanctuary
Redington Shores
North
Redington Beach
Redington Beach

Seminole

Pinellas
Park

Madeira Beach
John's Pass Village
& Boardwalk

(693)

(275)

Kopsick Palm
Arboretum

Boca Ciega

Planetarium &
Observatory

Coliseum
Ballroom
Sunken Gardens

Haas
Museum
Museum
of Fine Arts

Treasure Island

South
Pasadena

Historical
Museum

Gulfport

Bayfront Center
Great
Exploration
Salvador Dali
Museum

(19)

Lake Maggiore Park

St. Petersburg Beach
Silas' Wax Museum
& Funhouse

PINELLAS BAYWAY

Boyd Hill
Nature Trail

Pass-A-Grille
Beach

Tierra
Verde

Pinellas Point

Gulf of Mexico

(699)

ST. PETERSBURG

SUNSHINE SKYWAY BRIDGE

Cabbage
Key

Mullet Key

0   5   10 km
0   5 miles

Fort DeSoto Park

TAMPA AND ST. PETERSBURG

Lutz

275

41

75

301

Keystone Lake

Lake Magdalene

Citrus Park

Carrollwood

Lake Carroll

University of Southern Florida

Thonotosassa

TAMPA

Museum of Science and Industry
Adventure Island

Busch Gardens/
Dark Continent

Temple Terrace

Lowry Park Zoo

583

Rocky Creek

HILLSBOROUGH

AVENUE

92

Dover

Hillsborough River

Mango

4

Tampa
International Airport

Tampa Stadium

Ybor City

275

Henry B. Plant Museum

Tampa Museum of Art

CROSSTOWN EXPRESSWAY

60

Brandon

92

Harbour Island

McKay Bay

75

FRANKLAND BRIDGE

Progress Village

GANDY BRIDGE

685

Hillsborough Bay

41

Alafia

Riverview

MacDill
Air Force Base

Gibsonton

Gadsden Point

301

Bullfrog Creek

T a m p a

B a y

TAMIAMI TRAIL

672

Apollo Beach

Bahia Beach

674

Ruskin

Sun City Center

Wimauma

Sun City

75

41

Little Manatee

Piney Point

TAMPA

With an airport which is more efficient than Miami's, with the Pinellas resorts within easy driving range as well as the theme parks of the Orlando area, it is not surprising that the state's western portion has become so popular. Tampa has recently been nudging its way into position as a major cruise ship terminal – over $177 million was spent to deepen the port's main channel and $1.3 million was spent on Garrison Channel Cruise Ship Terminal. More money has been earmarked for a downtown terminal, complete with restaurants, shops and a hotel.

Tampa was listed as a Native American settlement by early mapmaker Fontenado in 1580 and shown on de Laet's map of 1625. When Spanish explorer De Soto landed here in 1539, however, it was known as Espiritu Santo Bay. Tampa was established as an American settlement in 1823 when Fort Brooke was built; but as troops left to join the Confederacy in 1861, it was left with a dwindling population.

The new communications of the 1880s brought people and power back to Tampa, including Spanish and Cuban immigrants who moved here to work for the cigar manufacturing industry in the district known as Ybor City. When phosphate was discovered, the port proved beneficial to its export. Henry Plant saw the town's potential as a winter tourist resort and, in eager competition with Flagler's east coast successes, built the Tampa Bay Hotel in 1891 (see **Museums**). This century, Tampa has seen some resurgence as a vacation destination. In keeping with this image, the Tampa Performing Arts Center, a three-theater complex on the banks of the Hillsborough River, is helping to make Tampa a major center for the arts. The $140 million Tampa Convention Center, comprising five hotels, opened in 1990, and more projects are afoot, including developments on Harbour Island which by 1994 will feature the Florida Aquarium at its eastern end. Meanwhile, Lowry Park Zoo, to the northwest, is adding exhibits to double its size, including a manatee center. Tampa is both sporty and festive. The Cincinnati Reds and other major baseball league teams carry out their spring training here and the autumn brings football with the Tampa Bay Buccaneers and the Hall of Fame Bowl. Being by the Bay, there are opportunities for motor boating, wind surfing or taking out a hobie cat (small catamaran). As for the festivals, Tampa is at its liveliest during the annual revelry of the Gasparilla Festival in January/February and when it hosts the State Fair in February. During the berry season (early March), there's a strawberry fest in neighboring Plant City and in Brandon, a Balloon Festival each October.

The Python slithers along a hair-raising route at Busch Gardens

WHAT TO SEE IN AND AROUND TAMPA

◆◆◆
BUSCH GARDENS/DARK CONTINENT

Busch Boulevard and 40th St.
This 300-acre (121-hectare) African-themed park appeals to all ages, featuring thrill rides, live entertainment, animal shows and exhibits, shops, restaurants and games. Over 3,000 animals are at home in seven distinctly themed sections. Busch Gardens is 6 miles (9.5km) from downtown Tampa, and 1¼ hours' drive from Orlando. The family center began about 30 years ago as a bird garden and hospitality house for Anheuser-Busch's Tampa brewery.
Today it is recognized as one of America's top zoos with the added attraction of rides like the African Queen boat cruise and the Scorpion and Python roller coasters. The center also fosters the propagation and

conservation of a variety of species, particularly those which are endangered. Four out of five Asian elephants born in captivity in North America have been born at Busch Gardens, for example, and there is a special nursery for newborn animals, with large viewing windows for park guests.

Visitors enter the park via the Morocco section where artisans can be watched at work, and their wares examined. Designed to resemble a typical walled Moroccan city, with elaborate tile work, snake charmers and belly dancers, this section offers several shows; some, such as a spectacular ice show, are performed in the 1,200-seat Moroccan Palace Theatre. The next section is Nairobi, home to the animal nursery, the Nairobi Train Station, a petting zoo and Nocturnal Mountain – a display of night creatures in a "night time" setting so that visitors may view their natural behavior. Part of this sector of the park is a 1-acre (0.4-hectare) elephant exhibit, a simulated version of the animals' natural habitat amid rock formations, greenery, waterfalls and a swimming hole. Elephant rides are available.

Serengeti Plain may be viewed from the new monorail, sky ride, steam locomotive or west promenade. Over 500 native African animals roam freely on this veldt-like plain including impala, giraffes and zebras. Display areas recently added accommodate elephants, Nile crocodiles, dromedary camels, Chilean flamingos and ostriches.

Timbuktu features thrilling rides – looping roller coasters, a boat swing ride, the Sandstorm thrill ride and the Carousel Caravan with camels and Arabian steeds. This section also features dolphin shows, a shopping bazaar, an electric games arcade and a German themed dining and entertainment complex.

Past this quarter lies the Congo, one of the most action-packed sections of the park. This is where you can take a white water raft ride, the

Several hours are needed to sample all the Busch Gardens activities

Monstrous Mamba or Swinging Vines rides. A unique feature here is Claw Island, displaying rare white tigers in a natural habitat.

In lively Stanleyville, visitors can browse through African crafts, watch a variety show, take a log flume ride or the tamer cruise boat ride, and observe free flying birds, watch the antics of the cockatoos in the Bird Gardens Theatre, see Eagle Canyon, where flightless golden and bald eagles reside, or take the children to the play area (parents could complete their time at Busch at the brewery, where complimentary beer is served). The newest attraction is Crown Colony an *Out of*

Africa themed area with plantation house and colonial restaurant. One entrance fee for Busch Gardens pays for all the park's activities.

Adjacent to the park **Adventure Island** is a separate, 22-acre water-themed park. Here one can take the Rambling Bayou, a leisurely float trip down a winding river; the 76ft (23m) high Tampa Typhoon free fall slide; the Gulf Stream speed slide; the Everglides toboggan slide or the Barratuba inner tube slide. Flume slides and pools are also available.

◆◆
MUSEUMS
Art and cultural exhibits frequently change at the **Tampa Museum of Art** on Doyle Carlton Drive. Across the Hillsborough River, the administrative offices of the University of Tampa are part of Henry Plant's exotic Tampa Bay Hotel, and Victorian era art, furniture and fashion are displayed in the **Henry B Plant Museum** off the lobby. Near Adventure Island, the **Museum of Science and Industry** involves visitor participation in its exhibits.

◆◆
YBOR CITY
This is Tampa's historic Latin Quarter, with wrought-iron balconies, plazas and arcades, and sidewalk cafés. Tampa flourished after Vicente Martinez Ybor moved his cigar-rolling factory here from Key West in the 1800s. Cubans were hired to work in the factories, hundreds of them

rolling cigars by hand.
The old factory has since
become Ybor Square, with
shops and theaters, but its
story is told at the **Ybor City
State Museum**, and you can
still buy a hand-rolled cigar
here (see **Shopping**).

Accommodations

Large hotels and short-term
rental apartments are
plentiful. All the big chain
names are here, including a
Hyatt Regency, Marriott,
Holiday Inn and Hilton. A
boat or helicopter will
transport visitors to Bahia
Beach Island Resort and
Marina in Tampa Bay, a full
service resort with hotel
rooms and apartments and a
range of sports.

Children

The treat for youngsters is
Tampa's own theme park,
Busch Gardens/Dark
Continent or the Lowry Park
Zoo; but Tampa is also an
excellent base for the Pinella
resorts or the Orlando area.
Many parents view it as an
ideal part of a two-center
holiday.

Restaurants

The wide range includes those
offering first class seafood and
those with a view of the Bay.
Ybor City offers Cuban/Spanish
cuisine and strong black coffee.
Another popular eating area is
The Market on Harbour Island
where you'll find speciality
shops, dining and dancing
establishments all leading to the
Waterwalk. Harbour Island may
be reached via two bridges or
the elevated People Mover
shuttle.

Shopping

The more unusual boutiques
can be found on Harbour
Island. At Ybor Square,
refurbished factory buildings
enclose shops selling a wide
range of antiques, imports, arts
and collectables. Other
shopping centers include the
Tampa Bay Center, University
Square Mall, West Shore Plaza,
Belz Factory Outlet and
upmarket Old Hyde Park
Village.

The Kapok Tree Restaurant gardens near Tampa

WHAT TO SEE ELSEWHERE IN FLORIDA

AMELIA ISLAND
north of Jacksonville.
This island is the most southerly of what Floridians refer to as the Golden Isles, at the entrance to the St Mary's River, a combination of lush oak glades and palmetto with salt marsh and rolling sand dunes. In 1686 it was known as Santa Maria with a Spanish post at what is now Fernandina Beach. South Carolina's governor, James Moore, attacked the island with an English force and Native American allies in 1702, captured the post and destroyed the Mission, and there were so many subsequent attacks that by 1730 Amelia was all but deserted.

It acquired its present name in 1735 when General James Oglethorpe re-established a post here, naming it after English King George II's sister, Princess Amelia. When Florida was returned to Spain in 1783, a large tract of the island's land was given to Don Domingo Fernandez, including a village named Fernandina in his honor. It became the haunt of pirates and smugglers in the 19th century.

Fernandina Beach is today's main reason for a visit, a colorful old port with a restored historic district downtown where gas lamps light up Victorian homes and visitors are invited to bend an elbow over the hand carved antique bar of a 19th-century saloon. Guides offer walking tours of the historic district and the island's rich history is best explained at the **Amelia Island Museum of History** on South Third Street.

Also of historic note is **Fort Clinch State Park**. Construction of the fort was begun in 1847, one in a chain built along the Atlantic coast, but was never completed. It was seized by Confederate troops in 1861 and abandoned in 1862 to Union troops, who used it as a prison. Nowadays, there are guided tours through the site and museum, special activities and recreational facilities on the grounds.

APALACHICOLA
Northwest Florida.
This town lies at the mouth of the Apalachicola River and is almost completely surrounded by water. It produces around 90 percent of the state's oysters from thousands of acres of oyster beds.

In town, the major point of interest is the **John Gorrie Museum**, named after a resident doctor who invented an ice-making machine in the 1840s which was to be the forerunner of the air conditioner and compression refrigerator. Gorrie invented his machine to cool the rooms of malaria patients but, although he patented the device in 1851, could not raise the money to develop it commercially. He died in 1855 without ever having gained recognition for his work.

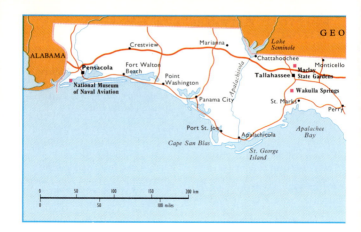

Within the Apalachicola
National Forest is **Fort
Gadsden State Historic Site**,
once a fort held by Native
Americans and runaway slaves
against US forces. In the park
you can picnic, fish, boat or
take the nature trail. Also within
the forest's boundaries is the
**St Mark's National Wildlife
Refuge**, a paradise for
ornithologists. **Apalachicola
National Forest** comprises
more than ½ a million acres
(0.2 million hectares),
spreading west from
Tallahassee to the river.
Wildlife is plentiful and there
are excellent spots to camp,
fish or swim.

◆◆
BOCA RATON
Palm Beach County.
The name may mean "mouth
of the rat" but this Gold Coast
resort is lively and attractive, a
center for the privileged. The
Spanish gave the site its name
because of the many sharp

and jagged rocks, like teeth,
just below the surface at this
point of the coast. These, in
combination with the domed
thatched Native American huts
they saw near the beach, led to
the nickname "rats' nests."
Eccentric architect Addison
Mizner envisioned Boca Raton
as his dream city in the 1920s –
an American Venice, since at
the time a grand canal was
etched down the main
thoroughfare to the sea
(nowadays El Camino Real).
The town was a shipping center
for winter fruit and vegetables,
until Mizner decided to
decorate the canal with
ornamental landings and
Venetian style bridges, and, in
keeping with this theme,
transport visitors by electric
gondola.
Mizner's dream was never
really fulfilled – the toppling of
Florida's land boom saw to that
– but the hotel he designed in
1925 to be the "flossiest hotel
around," has survived. The

FLORIDA

GEORGIA

ATLANTIC

OCEAN

Amelia Island

Osceola
National Forest

Jacksonville

Jacksonville
Beach

Lake
City

Orange
Park

Castillo de San Marcos
St. Augustine
Alligator Farm

Lightner Museum

Gainesville

Marineland

Palatka

St. John's River

Suwannee

Ormond Beach
Daytona Beach

Lake
George

Silver Springs

Ocala
National
Forest

Ocala

De Land

Cedar Key

Leesburg

Homosassa Springs

Sanford

Cape Canaveral National Seashore

Weeki Wachee

Orlando

Titusville
J.F. Kennedy Space Center/
Spaceport USA
Cape Canaveral

Disney World
& EPCOT Center
Sea World
Circus World

Dade City

Tarpon Springs

Rockledge

Cocoa Beach

Lakeland

Winter
Haven

Clearwater

Tampa

Melbourne

Cypress
Gardens

Lake
Wales

FLORIDA TURNPIKE

Lake
Kissimmee

St. Petersburg

Tampa Bay

Bradenton

Ringling Museum
Jungle Gardens

Bellm's Cars &
Music of Yesterday
Sarasota

Sebring

Lake
Placid

Peace

Intracoastal Waterway

Fort Pierce

Port Charlotte

Lake
Okeechobee

Jupiter

Caloosahatchee

West Palm Beach
Palm Beach

Cape Coral

Fort Myers
Edison's Home

Belle Glade

Deerfield Beach

Boca Raton
Pompano Beach
Fort Lauderdale
Ocean World
Dania Beach
Hollywood

Naples

ALLIGATOR ALLEY

The

Everglades

Marco Island

Everglades City

Miami Beach
Miami

Weeks Air Museum
Monkey Jungle
Fruit & Spice Park
Everglades
National Park
Cape Sable
Mangrove
Swamp

Metrozoo
Orchid Jungle
Coral Castle
Florida City

Gulf of Mexico

Flamingo

Florida Bay

Key Largo

Islamorada

Dry Tortugas

Long Key

Big Pine Key

Florida Keys

Marathon

Straits of Florida

Key West

Florida

WHAT TO SEE

Coastal wildlife can be seen at Cape Canaveral National Seashore

original was named the Cloister Inn, a hostelry that has since been expanded, embellished and developed into the glossy and giant Boca Raton Hotel and Club. Since then, too, golf courses, condominiums, villas and vacation homes, shopping complexes and marinas have all sprouted in the vicinity. Speciality restaurants and Spanish-styled shops, dinner theaters and winter polo games, not to mention the beach itself, all help to give this base a plush and monied air.

◆
CAPE CANAVERAL NATIONAL SEASHORE
South of New Smyrna Beach, this seashore extends for 25 miles (40km). At the southern end, Playalinda Beach is good for swimming and surfing. The central position has remained undeveloped, a place to look for giant loggerhead and green turtles among the dunes and sea oats. In the summer, the turtles crawl ashore to lay their eggs. Climb the boardwalk to Turtle Mound, where for centuries the Native Americans piled up shells.

◆
COCOA BEACH
Central east coast.
An oceanfront resort with an expanse of white sand fronted by hotels, restaurants and bars. See the **Patrick Air Force Base Missile Display**, which has a collection of rockets and other space vehicles, and the **Brevard Art Center and**

Museum where exhibits
constantly change (closed
Monday). The community of
Cocoa itself is across the Indian
River on the Intracoastal
Waterway, connecting with the
Atlantic.

DADE CITY
A small but charming
community south of Bushnell on
US301, Dade City has a southern
air with its azalea blooms and
moss-draped oaks and
camphor trees. This is basically
an *en route* stop to the **Dade
Battlefield State Historic
Site**, where an 1835 Native
American ambush sparked off
the seven-year-long Seminole
Wars. The 80-acre park is a
memorial to Major Francis
Dade and his men who died
here. These days there are only
nature trails and picnic spots.

DANIA BEACH
Dania.
A 2-mile (3km) palm-shaded
strip of public beach not far
from Miami. It used to be
known as the "Antique Centre
of the South" and there are still
"finds" to be made, but no
bargains! Just to the north on
A1A, the **John U Lloyd Beach
State Recreation Area** is a
partially-developed barrier
island providing visitors with
places to fish, swim and boat.

◆◆
DAYTONA BEACH
Central east coast.
Best known for its International
Speedway and that perennial
main event in February, the
Daytona 500. Other big races

include the Pepsi 400 each July,
and motorcycle races every
March and October. This is a
top resort along Florida's
central east coast, an area
originally inhabited by the
Timucuan Indians. The first
permanent settlement was
made in 1870 by an Ohio man
named "Day." Daytona first
became associated with motor
racing because its beach
proved ideal for the sport –
500ft (150m) wide, with 23
miles (37km) of hard white
sand smoothed by incoming
tides. Alexander Winton broke
the world record here in 1903
at a speed of 68mph (109kph),
and many wealthy racing
enthusiasts were attracted to
the area. The **Birthplace of
Speed Museum**, Ormond
Beach, celebrates the early
days of car racing here and
exhibits include a 1922 Model-
T. Closed Sunday and Monday.
Motor racing apart, Daytona is
a fun-packed vacation resort
with fairs and amusements
centered on **Forest
Amusement Park**, bordering
the beach and boardwalk. For
the best view, climb to the top
of the 176ft (54m) Space
Needle. The Museum of Arts
and Sciences (closed
Mondays) includes history
displays and a planetarium,
and for relaxation there are
sightseeing cruises to Ponce de
Leon Inlet, its historic
lighthouse and nearby islands.

◆
DEERFIELD BEACH
Located just south of Boca
Raton and bordering the
Everglades region of the

WHAT TO SEE

Oxahatchee Recreation Area, where airboat rides and fishing are available, Deerfield Beach's highlight is its **Island Park**, accessible only by boat – a tiny island in the Intracoastal Waterway. Today this is a great spot for fishing and bird watching, but it used to be notorious as the hideout of Chicago gangster Al Capone.

Of interest in the town is the restored Old Schoolhouse, housing memorabilia from the 1920s, and Pioneer House, built of pine and a typical example of "Cracker" architecture.

DE LAND
Central east coast.
Founded by and named after Henry Deland in 1876, this is a good base for nature lovers heading for nearby wilderness areas. An attractive town with oak-lined streets, De Land hosts many events during the year, the most popular of which is the annual Artists Sidewalk Art Festival, which, in March, attracts participants from all over the country.
The main site of interest lies 6 miles (9½km) north: **De Leon Springs**, discovered by Ponce de Leon in 1513. The springs form a subterranean stream pouring out a staggering 94,000 gallons of water every minute. They are surrounded by a well-shaded area rich in birdlife, Native American burial grounds and recreational facilities. Boat tours of St John's River are available not far from De Land and there's a ferry to

nearby Hontoon Island.

DELRAY BEACH
The main attraction of this resort near Miami is **Morikami Park**, with its ½-mile (0.8km) self-guided nature trail and Museum of Japanese Culture, donated to the county by the last survivor of the Yamato colony of Japanese pineapple farmers.
Loxahatchee National Wildlife Refuge, with a recreation area at either end, is only 13 miles (21km) northwest.

THE EVERGLADES
Most of Florida's southern tip belongs to the Everglades National Park, comprising well over a million acres (0.4 million hectares) of marshland and sawgrass ruled by wildlife and for the most part left untouched. Indeed, it was never explored at all until the middle of the 19th century, when soldiers were sent in search of the remaining Seminoles, and attempts to reclaim the swamp were first made in 1903. There are several ways to enjoy the Everglades, but remember that the area is vast; don't expect to see more than a small section. Sightseeing excursions are made here from Florida's main vacation centers but visitors traveling independently can pick up a free map and information at the Visitor Center at the main entrance. For drivers' convenience, there is a paved road through the heart of the park, stopping at Flamingo. Stop once in a while

The anhinga, or "snake-bird," sunbathes in its Everglades home

and take to the boardwalks – but don't leave them; parts of the Everglades have remained uncharted and any alligators you see are not the Disney kind! Hiking enthusiasts may certainly reach the center of the park on foot, but perhaps the most enjoyable way of seeing this mangrove wilderness is by boat – canoe, airboat, or even houseboat. Only a small part of the Pahokee (Native American for "grassy waters") River runs through the Everglades. An English surveyor had dubbed the area River Glades but the "ever" was tacked on and has been used since the 19th century. The area's wealth of bird and animal life, vegetation and waterways has made it one of the state's greatest national treasures. Six hundred varieties of fish, 300 species of birds, countless mammals and 45 indigenous plant species are said to be found here. You should soon begin to recognize strangler figs, black racer snakes, wood storks, native orchids and gumbo-limbo trees, given time to explore. Hammocks – small islands of hardwood trees and shrubs – are scattered throughout the swamps, and dense thickets on the higher ground have probably been created by oaks, coco plums and custard apple trees, while the cypress is the most familiar vegetation on the lower ground.

Visitors entering at the southern gate (the location of the Royal Palm Visitor Center) soon reach Long Pine Key, where there is a 7-mile (11km) nature trail, campsites and picnic areas. This base leads to the Pa-hay-okee Overlook observation tower and Mahogany Hammock Trail. Canoeists might try the Noble Hammock Trail but only the experienced should attempt the Hell's Bay Trail.

Even the less hardy can take advantage of the walking trails,

Elevated boardwalks offer close views of the Everglades wildlife

which start from a ½-mile (0.8km) excursion to much longer distances. The Anhinga Trail, for instance, named after one of the native birds, stretches for just 1½ miles (2.5km) along a raised boardwalk over the sawgrass; and the adjacent Gumbo Limbo Trail is a mere ½ mile (0.8km), winding through a hammock. The Pineland Trail, on the other hand, is 6½ miles (10.5km) long – but this is a good one for spotting some of the lovely orchids; and the Pa-hay-okee Trail, at 12½ miles (20km), does require stamina to complete.

Many Everglades visitors head for the developed tourist section at Flamingo where, these days, there are accommodations, marine stores and a marina, though Flamingo was once an isolated fishing village accessible only by boat. The easy way to explore the surroundings is to take a tour boat from here passing Coot Bay, along the Buttonwood Canal and visiting Tarpon Creek before reaching Cape Sable where you can go ashore and take the Wilderness Train through mangrove forests and Snake Bight Trail.

Tram tours of the park start at Shark Valley and sightseeing tours by boat of the Ten Thousand Islands area start near Everglades City. These islands of mangrove trees (quite a tangle) lie off the coast of Marco Island and the Everglades, and are formed from shell, driftwood and seaweed trapped in the

Canals and inlets wind through Fort Lauderdale

mangrove roots. As the trees mature they topple into the water and take root again, so new islands are constantly being formed.

♦♦♦
FORT LAUDERDALE
Southeast Florida.
The "Venice of America" has a touch of the Riviera, thanks to over 300 miles (483km) of lagoons, canals and rivers, and miles of Atlantic beaches. Named after Major William Lauderdale who built a fort here in 1838 during the Seminole Wars, Fort Lauderdale is a lively vacation center. Even in its early days, tourists flocked here, maybe for its abundance of bars, gambling halls and brothels, for at one time it was considered a "Sin City." Rum runners brought in liquor by the crate from the Bahamas to keep the early tourists happy – among them a man named Bill Macoy, a rum runner who only carried the best brands of liquor – "the real Macoy."

Tourists in the 1950s included droves of college students, who helped form the bright, youthful image of present day Fort Lauderdale. All the watersports ever devised are available, including diving and snorkelling on the offshore reefs. Boating is probably the most popular, and facilities for chartering and sailing are excellent. A favorite way to take in the sights is by old fashioned riverboat – perhaps on a dinner cruise. The **Jungle Queen** cruises leave from the Bahia Mar Yachting Center on day or evening trips; in the evenings there is a barbecue and shrimp dinner, a vaudeville show and a singalong. In the daytime the cruise passes Millionaire's Row, and passengers can disembark at the Seminole Indian Village. **Paddlewheel Queen** cruises leave from one block south of Oakland Park Beach Bridge and also offer day or night sailings.

Fort Lauderdale is actually the hub of an intricate inland boating paradise that extends throughout Broward County. Boaters on this section of the Intracoastal Waterway tend to be dedicated to life on the water, but others can experience it in any size or type of vessel for any length of time. For a look at the more glamorous boats, go to Pier 66 marina or Bahia Mar.

Water makes an impact in other

At anchor in Fort Lauderdale

ways. Children will enjoy **Ocean World** at SE 17th St Causeway, for example, where they will see sharks, sea lions, turtles, dolphin shows and an oceanarium featuring denizens of the deep. The **International Swimming Hall of Fame** (just behind the beach on Seabreeze Boulevard) not only hosts collegiate competitions but contains memorabilia from numerous nations and computerized displays. Restaurants in the area serve some of the best seafood, supplied by the Atlantic Ocean and the nearby Gulf of Mexico. The choice is endless – as it is for hotels and shops. The traditional place to shop is Las Olas Boulevard, which extends for about 1½ miles (2·5km) from downtown.

State and regional parks are countless, too. The closest is 180-acre (72-hectare) **Hugh Taylor Birch State Park**, across the street from the ocean. In **Himmarshee Village**, a one-room schoolhouse and the King-Cromartie House, furnished in turn-of-the-century style, may be toured.

The home of Fort Lauderdale's earliest white settlers is today a historical museum on Las Olas Boulevard – **Stranahan House** (open Wednesday and Friday to Sunday). But the museum not to be missed is the **Discovery Center**, on SW 2nd Avenue, built in 1905 as the New River Inn, and now a hands-on museum and science center especially appealing to children. Art lovers should head for the **Museum of Art**, opened in 1986 on Las Olas Boulevard. Its permanent collection includes Florida's largest collection of Oceanic, West African, preColumbian and Native American art. The best way to get to know the resort and its environs is to take the 18-mile (29km) trip by the **Voyager Train**, from South Seabreeze Boulevard, passing the residential areas and Port Everglades. Another enjoyable way to explore is by water-taxi, on demand like a land taxi (tel: (305) 565 5507) from any safe dock, or with an excursion ticket for a day's aimless cruising. Guided tours are also available.

◆
FORT PIERCE
Situated on US1 and Florida 68 on the west side of the saltwater Indian River (in reality a lagoon), Fort Pierce could be visited on the way to Cape Canaveral. For recreation, there are four public beaches and the **Fort Pierce Inlet/St Lucie Museum State Recreation Area** which also has a beach. The museum contains treasures from the deep; for a typical turn-of-the-century Floridian home and for native American artifact displays, look into the **St Lucie County Historical Museum** on Seaway Drive.

◆
FORT WALTON BEACH
Come to this lively playground of the northwest today and it's hard to believe that in 1910 black bears outnumbered people here! Make sure to bring along your fishing rod to try your hand at the area's most popular sport – coastal waters are teeming with fish. The pier stretches into the Gulf of Mexico for over 1,000ft (305m) and fishing possibilities range from trolling to surf or freshwater. Yachting, too, is another prime sport – many regattas take place at Fort Walton Beach.

In the center of the resort is the **Indian Temple Mound Museum**, a National Historic landmark depicting over 10,000 years of Gulf Coast living in the Choctawhatchee Bay area. Northeast of the city, Eglin Air Force Base offers tours which include its **Air Force Armament Museum**; and across the bridge on Okaloosa Island is the **Gulfarium**, a marine attraction with porpoise and sea lion shows, a Living Seas exhibit and huge tanks where marine life may be studied.

◆
GAINESVILLE
A possible *en route* stop to or from Jacksonville, Palatka or Ocala, this college town is located midway between the Atlantic and the Gulf. It was named in 1853 to honor General Edmund Gaines, a leader in the Seminole Wars – an improvement on the former title of Hog Town! Much of the activity revolves around the campus of what is now the University of Florida, such as the **Art Gallery** and **Teaching Gallery**, both on the university grounds. At one end, the **Lake Alice Wildlife Preserve** is worth strolling through.

The remains of Yulee Sugar Mill, built over a hundred years ago

◆
HOLLYWOOD
This beach resort is part of Broward County, close to Fort Lauderdale. Gift shops, cafés and restaurants all overlook the ocean along the Hollywood Beach boardwalk but its biggest attraction for families is **Six Flags Atlantis**, a watery theme park with a huge wave pool, slides, chutes and an 11-acre (4.4-hectare) lake. One entrance price pays for the whole thing, including live entertainment and waterski shows.
Topeekeegee Yugnee Recreation Area is a lakeside park with canoes and paddleboats for rent, bicycle trails and picnic sites; or sample the rides and water sport facilities in the newer **CB Smith Park**.

◆
HOMOSASSA SPRINGS
An ideal destination, 2 miles (3km) from Homosassa itself (a Native American name

meaning "the place of pepper trees"). Here you can wander through botanical gardens, visit the underwater observatory or cruise along tropical jungle waterways in a pontoon boat. The springs are natural deep water ones, pouring out about 70,000 gallons every minute to form a natural aquarium.

West of the springs, off US19, the **Yulee Sugar Mill Ruins** are in a state park, once part of a 5,000-acre plantation, the property of David Yulee, Florida's first US senator. To the south of Homosassa is the **Chassahowitzka National Wildlife Refuge**.

JACKSONVILLE

The largest, most commercial town in the northeast, named after President Andrew Jackson, sits on the banks of St John's River. The **Riverwalk** is pleasant to take, a route that lasts just over a mile (1.6km), bordered by shops and restaurants. **Jacksonville Landing** is a riverfront entertainment complex with upscale shops and restaurants, connected to the town by elevated light railway. This was one of the state's earliest settlements for both the French and Spanish, who built forts here. The walls of Fort Caroline have been reconstructed on the original 16th-century site, on what is now Fort Caroline Road and the **Fort Caroline National Memorial**.

Jacksonville has always thrived; the seafarers filled its Bay Street bars, and their schooners filled its harbor in the 19th century, and it became a popular winter resort after 1863 when the first theater and several large hotels opened. There are now several theaters in town, as well as a ballet troupe and symphony orchestra with a year-round schedule.

Downtown, the Friendship Park Fountain is illuminated at night and sprays water up to 120ft (36m) high. Jacksonville has a number of interesting museums: one of the best collections of porcelain to be found anywhere in the state is in the **Cummer Gallery of Art**, along with displays of modern art. Another fine contemporary collection is displayed at the **Jacksonville Art Museum** (closed Monday) on Boulevard Center Drive, while the **Museum of Science and Industry** on Gulf Life Drive, has scientific and anthropological displays, a planetarium and aquarium. The city's **Zoo** at 8605 Zoo Road is recommended for children; around 700 exotic and native animals can be seen in natural habitats in this 61-acre zoological park. They may be viewed from the elevated nature walkway or the miniature railway. For adults, the **Anheuser-Busch Brewery** on Busch Drive admits parties free to see the brewing and bottling process and sample the end product. Jacksonville's holiday resort section is **Jacksonville Beach**, whose focal point is the beach pier and boardwalk.

Wind and sand erosion has created these rock "alligators" dotted with blow-holes on Jupiter Island's Blowing Rocks Preserve

◆
JUPITER
Southeast Florida.
Once the home of actor Burt Reynolds, this is an excellent spot for windsurfing, and several international competitions take place here. The best view is from the **Jupiter Lighthouse**, a red brick landmark perched on a bluff, overlooking the Jupiter Inlet and the Gulf Stream. The lighthouse is still operational but is also a small museum containing local historic memorabilia. The waterfront is best for restaurant choice. Restful places to visit for wildlife are located to the north of Jupiter: **Hobe Sound National Wildlife Refuge** is reached via US1 – sea turtles nest on the beach here and nature trails are marked for hikers. The nearby **Jonathan Dickinson State Park** is a departure point for river boat tours and has canoes, bicycles and cabins for rent. The park takes its name from Jonathan Dickinson, who was shipwrecked here in 1696 and managed to stay alive until Native Americans finally drove him away, and he escaped to St Augustine.

◆◆
MARCO ISLAND
An offshore island which has become a west coast hot spot without losing its charm. Somewhat more remote than the more familiar populated areas, it nevertheless has resort hotels and villas, shops, wide beaches and wildlife, as well as the "Marco Moo Trolley" to take people around. The island was the home of the Calusa Indians from 500BC to AD1700, and important archaeological finds have been made here. Another reason to head for this destination is that it is close to the Everglades and the Ten Thousand Islands.

◆
MONTICELLO
Northwest Florida.
Those who have a penchant for the Deep South will feel an affinity for this town, named after Thomas Jefferson's Virginia home. It was founded by Georgia and Carolina planters in the early 1800s, and continues to be an agricultural district where watermelons, pecans and satsuma oranges are grown. Visitors come to admire the antebellum homes and plantations, the most famous of which is **Bellamy** on State 133. John Bellamy was one of the South Carolina planters who settled in this part of Florida, but he did more than plant fruit: he laid out Jacksonville and became one of the USA's wealthiest men.

◆◆
OCALA NATIONAL FOREST
These thousands of acres of wilderness have been nicknamed the "Big Scrub" due

to the numerous sand pine. Located east of Ocala (a region noted for horse farms) and stretching from Oklawaha to St John's River, the Forest is home to hundreds of deer and its streams are a haven for fishermen.

The two recreational bases are: Juniper Springs, 26 miles (42km) east of Ocala on State 40, where eight million gallons of water pour out every day at a warm temperature, and Alexander Springs, 16 miles (26km) north of Eustis off State 19, where over 70 million gallons of water flow daily. Both places are good for swimming and canoeing.

◆
OSCEOLA NATIONAL FOREST
Northeast Florida.
This expansive forest offers 157,000 acres for camping, fishing or exploring. One favorite base is Ocean Pond, though you could opt for Lake City at the forest edge. Osceola embraces the **Olustee Historic Battlefield Site**, where the only significant Civil War battle on Florida soil was fought. Worth seeing in February, when costumed participants come from all over the country to re-enact the 1864 Confederate victory.

◆◆
PALM BEACHES
Both Palm Beach and its neighbor West Palm Beach are élite resorts on Florida's Gold Coast, the haunts of well-heeled hedonists, where Rolls Royces and credit cards are at their most active.

Not until the Civil War was the first house built in Palm Beach – by a draft dodger – and by 1873 there were still no more than four families. It was probably due to an 1878 shipwreck, when coconuts were washed ashore, planted and bore fruit, that this uninspired site was first noticed. In 1880 the settlers decided on the name Palm City, but had to rechristen it Palm Beach, since the former already existed. The luxurious look of Palm Beach can be attributed to Addison Mizner, who designed Mediterranean-style homes for the wealthy – and, indeed, created a whole new industry in the area to produce the bright glazed tiles he wanted. The élitist reputation was, however, started by Henry Flagler, the railway mogul, who established Palm Beach as a playground for himself and his rich friends. His pioneer hotel, the Royal Poinciana, quickly became a favorite with Philadelphia society and their stamp of approval led to the construction of other opulent estates and exclusive clubs. Flagler's own white marble palatial mansion on Whitehall Way, off Coconut Row, has become the **Henry Morrison Flagler Museum**, restored to its 1902 grandeur with Flagler's own private railroad car The Rambler a permanent exhibit in the estate's grounds (museum closed Monday).

In West Palm Beach, the **Norton Gallery of Art** on South Olive Avenue has a

*The Palm Beach house built by
Henry Flagler for his third wife
(above and detail, right) is now a
museum named after the mogul*

particularly fine collection of
jade (closed Monday); and in
the **South Florida Science
Museum** on Dreher Trail,
there are hands-on exhibits in
the Discovery Hall, samples of
underwater life in the
Aquarium, and a planetarium.
Travel west on Southern
Boulevard to reach **Lion
Country Safari**, where the big
cats and other African wildlife
roam uncaged. Elephant and
boat rides, campgrounds and a
hospitality center are all part of

the complex. The **Dreher Park Zoo** on Summit Boulevard features animals, gardens and nature trails.

The Palm Beaches are noted for their deluxe hotels, such as The Breakers, and quality stores, such as those lining Worth Avenue in the heart of Palm Beach. The glitterati come to watch polo – British royalty has played here – and are whisked around by Rolls Royces or Bentleys, to dinner at the Poinciana Club or to the show at the Royal Poinciana Playhouse.

◆
PANAMA CITY

Located about 100 miles (160km) east of Pensacola on St Andrew's Bay, this is not only an important commercial port city but a vibrant resort town. Panama City Beach is 30 miles (48km) away across the bay, where there is a whirlwind of constant activity. Children love the **Miracle Strip Amusement Park**, which adds new rides and attractions each year and includes a giant roller coaster. At **Gulf World** near the pier, there are several daily animal shows, underwater exhibits and a dolphin petting pool. At **Snake-A-Torium** you can learn all about venom extraction and meander around a tropical garden. Other attractions include **Shipwreck Island**, a water theme park on the Miracle strip. The **Museum of Man in the Sea**, on Black Beach Road, is all about the history of underwater exploration.
For a fascinating day's excursion, take one of the half-hour boat tours from Captain Anderson's Pier and Treasure Island Marina to **Shell Island**, a barrier island where you can shell, sunbathe, snorkel or swim; or visit **St Andrews State Recreation Area**, at the eastern tip of Panama City Beach, where there are wide beaches, dunes, wildlife and a restored "cracker" or pioneer turpentine still, as well as nature trails, camping and plenty of sports facilities. Accommodations range from campsites to resort properties and hotels with kitchen facilities. Shopping includes a mall carved out of the "mountain" attraction, Alvin's Magic Mountain, with restaurants and game rooms as well.

◆◆
PENSACOLA

Northwest Florida.
They call it the "city of five flags," and Pensacola has been under the rule of different flags since 1559. This is one of Florida's most historic cities, though today it is a flourishing industrial center with a naval station and large, natural landlocked harbor, on the north shore of the Bay. To the east, Bayou Texar and, to the west, Bayou Chico are the wide arms of the bay which reach inland each side of the Pensacola peninsula. Recorded history begins with Captain Maldonado, commander of the fleet which took De Soto to Florida. The name could stem from the Spanish seaport Peniscola; or from the Native

American words *panshi*
("hair") and *okla* ("people") –
once the nickname for the
long-haired people who lived
here. History and heritage are
today's attractions, no more so
than in the **Pensacola
Historic Village**, where
visitors can tour through
restored homes, art galleries,
antique shops and museums.
The oldest church in Florida is
the **Pensacola Historical
Museum** on South Adams
Street, and what used to be the
old city jail is now the
Pensacola Museum of Art
on Jefferson Street (closed
Sunday and Monday).
The **North Hill Preservation
District** is a 50-block area
where homes and other
buildings from the 18th and
19th centuries have been
restored. **Seville Historic
District**, too, is worth
exploring, with restaurants and
speciality shops scattered
between the historic homes.
The old commercial heart of
the city is contained in the
Palafox Historic District.
The original city square was
Plaza Ferdinand and one of the
unique houses close to the
square was Walton House,
designed in French West
Indies style. A short walk away
is the **West Florida Museum
of History** and, across the
street, the **Transportation
Museum** looks like a
Pensacola street as it was at the
turn of the century: paved in
brick and flanked with wooden
sidewalks, and including a
trolley car, gas station and
several small shops selling
"olde worlde" merchandise

such as heirloom clothing and
tin plate photographs.
Across from Plaza Ferdinand,
on Jefferson Street, the
Pensacola City Hall houses the
TT Wentworth Museum –
the region's first proper
museum with a vast collection
of over 30,000 items of local
historic interest including a
Coca Cola collection and
hands-on "Discovery"
exhibition for children to
enjoy.
West of town is the Naval Air
Station, where the first Navy
flyers were trained for World
War 1 combat. The **National
Museum of Naval Aviation**
has aircraft from the dawn of
flight to a replica of the Skylab
Command Module, plus
aviation memorabilia – and it's
free. Nearby is the 16th-
century Spanish **Fort
Barrancas**, part of the Gulf
Islands National Seashore (see
below), and the old Pensacola
Lighthouse.
Across the Bay, **Pensacola
Beach**, on Santa Rosa Island,
offers sugar-white sands and a
busy nightlife. **Fort Pickens**,
at the island's western tip, saw
Civil War action, and served
as a prison for Geronimo, and
is today part of the Gulf Islands
National Seashore, 150 square
miles (240sq km) of islands
and keys, much of which is
state protected. Here you can
see wildlife – and even find a
beach area to yourself
(recommended for surfers).
For a striking view of Santa
Rosa Island and the Gulf,
climb the observation tower in
**Big Lagoon State
Recreation Area**, a popular

woodland summer spot with an open air auditorium where concerts are held.
At unspoiled **Perdido Key** (situated half-way between Pensacola and Mobile, Alabama) a quiet day out can be spent at Johnson's Beach, where there's room to spread out.

◆
POMPANO BEACH
This resort is easily reached from neighboring Fort Lauderdale, but also has its own choice of hotels, restaurants and nightclubs. Many of its shops are concentrated around Fashion Square at 23rd Street, an airy mall which is well landscaped and adorned with fine sculpture.
Alternatively, try Ocean Side Center, a few yards from the beach. Among family activities is **Waterboggan**, north of Fashion Square – Florida's first mountain waterslide.

The USA's oldest house: Gonzalez-Alvarez House, St Augustine

◆◆◆
ST AUGUSTINE
Northeast Florida.
America's oldest city, St Augustine was first discovered by Ponce de Leon in 1513, but named by Don Pedro Menendez de Aviles in 1565. It became Spain's North American military headquarters and for many years served as Florida's capital. The city was attacked and captured many times, but despite a severe campaign launched by Sir Francis Drake in 1586, the British did not claim it until 1763, after which great plantations were established. After 1900, its residential population was swelled by European immigrants, particularly from the island of Menorca. Visitors are encouraged to take the 7-mile (11.3km) tour of the city by horse-drawn carriage or sightseeing train, which can be left and rejoined at will, and perhaps take a cruise of the waterfront. In the oldest quarter, San Augustin Antiguo (the city's original name), costumed artisans demonstrate the crafts of an earlier era and the narrow streets and restored buildings reflect the Spanish heritage. There is no better place to start a tour than at the **Fountain of Youth Park** on Magnolia Avenue, a memorial to Ponce de Leon, who came to Florida in search of the elusive elixir of youth. Flagler's old Alcazar Hotel on King Street is today the **Lightner Museum**, housing superb examples of Tiffany glass as well as mechanical musical instruments and other antiques. **Oldest House**, on narrow St Francis Street, is a structure combining Spanish, British and American influences. **Oldest Schoolhouse** on St George Street, built of red cedar and cypress clamped together with wooden pegs, is believed to have been built during the Spanish occupation; while

WHAT TO SEE

Oldest Store on Artillery Lane would have been a community meeting place in the 1800s. For those who are interested in American history there is a great deal to see – more than 70 sites in the historic district. Others of note are **Casa de Hidalgo**, furnished in the style of early 17th-century Spain; **De Mesa Sanchez House**, an old Spanish inn; the old Ponce de Leon Hotel, now the **Flagler College**; and **Flagler Memorial Presbyterian Church**, built by Flagler in 1889. The Spanish built St Augustine's ornate cathedral in the 1790s; also of religious interest is the **Shrine of Nuestra Senora de la Leche**. Dominating the entrance to Matanzas Bay is the **Castillo de San Marcos**, North America's oldest masonry fort (begun 1672) with splendid views of the old quarter and City Gate from its walls. Fourteen miles (22½km) south of the city, on Rattlesnake Island, **Fort Matanzas** was the site of the bloody 16th-century struggle between French and Spanish colonists, resulting in the slaughter (*matanzas*) of 300 French Huguenots. Museums on the lighter side, recommended for children, include the **Wax Museum** on St Marco Avenue. **St Augustine Alligator Farm**,

Castillo de San Marcos, built from shellrock in the 17th century

the state's oldest attraction, with hundreds of alligators and crocodiles and hourly "shows," and **Marineland**, with continuous dolphin shows, are both on Route A1A South. Nature lovers should head out to **Faver-Dykes**, the marshy and wooded acreage overlooking Matanzas River and Pellicer Creek, with nature trails and facilities for boating, fishing and picnicking. A

Henry Flagler's memorial to his daughter: the Presbyterian Church

favorite oceanside park at St Augustine Beach is the **Anastasia Recreation Area** – acres of beaches, dunes and a lagoon.

SINGER ISLAND
A delightful spot, only a 15-minute drive north of Palm

Beach, but not such an expensive place to stay. The proximity of the Gulf Stream keeps temperatures constant – cooler in summer and warmer in winter than many other parts of the state. The beautiful, wide public beach is a big draw and all types of watersports are available.

◆◆◆
SARASOTA

A cultural city 53 miles (85km) south of Tampa, Sarasota may be reached via the scenic route along Gulf Drive from the barrier islands, or the faster I75.

There is a choice of white sands, not only on the offshore islands but at the bays and small inlets indenting the coast. The city itself has its own brand of charm, enough to have tempted circus entrepreneur John Ringling to build his dream home here: Ca'D'Zan and its 38-acre (15.4-hectare) estate is today part of the **Ringling Museum Complex**. The Ringlings amassed magnificent tapestries and art works which can now be seen at the estate's Art Museum, though undoubtedly children will prefer the Gallery of the Circus. Also on the site is the Asolo Theater, an 18th-century Italian theater dismantled by Ringling, brought to the US and reconstructed here in 1950. Across from the Ringling Museums, **Bellm's Cars and Music of Yesterday** contains a fascinating collection of vintage cars, nickelodeons, phonographs and antique

games. In the **Sarasota Jungle Gardens** on Bayshore Road, visitors can look out for alligators, mina birds, macaws, and flamingos amid thousands of palms and flowering shrubs.

Fishing is highly regarded in the Sarasota vicinity, whether from a beach, a boat or in the **Myakka River State Park**, a wildlife reserve about 14 miles (22½km) east of town on Florida 72. A paved road

Ca'D'Zan, the exotic Ringling house

winds through most of the park, a train operates to the bird observation tower, and guided boat tours may be taken.

◆
TALLAHASSEE
This state capital city's native American name means "old town." Situated 30 miles (48km) north of the Gulf of Mexico, midway between Pensacola and Jacksonville, Tallahassee was a flourishing Apalachee Indian settlement in 1539 when De Soto arrived. The site of the former Native American village and Spanish Mission is currently the **San Luis Archaeological Site** on Mission Road (guided tours Sunday).

The atmosphere is very southern – the city was never captured during the Civil War – and there are many fine mansions and plantations. One of the oldest houses is **The Columns** at the junction of North Adam Street and West Park Street, constructed of red brick with a pitch roof and columned entrance. Guides will claim that a nickel is

The capital complex, Tallahassee, Florida's capital since 1823

knoll overlooking the business district. On Mondays, Wednesdays and Fridays, tours may be made of the **Governor's Mansion**, patterned after Andrew Jackson's Tennessee home, The Hermitage. Historic artifacts and treasures may be viewed at the **Museum of Florida History** on Bronough Street. For younger visitors, the **Tallahassee Junior Museum**, near the airport, features nature trails and an 1880 pioneer farm, and is also a refuge for the endangered Florida panther.

Winter is probably the best time to see **Alfred B Maclay State Ornamental Gardens** (north of town on US319, when azaleas and other native flowers are in full bloom. South of town, off SR61, at **Wakulla Springs**, thousands of gallons of water flow each minute from underground caverns to form the Wakulla River, upon which glass-bottom boat rides are offered. **Lake Jackson Mounds State Archaeological Site** on the shore of Lake Jackson is small but of interest to historians – it was here that the first Christmas Mass in the New World was held in 1539, and many Native American temple mounds have also been uncovered here. Tallahassee is also the location of one of Florida's few vineyards, Lafayette Vineyards & Winery on Mahan Drive, where tours and tastings are available.

embedded into every brick, but no one has torn the house down to prove it. More feasible is the story that the mahogany staircase connecting the rear hall to the upper floor was built through the rich owner's bedroom to prevent his lovely daughter leaving without his knowledge! Sightseers should not miss a tour of the old **State Capitol** (1902), situated beside the new (1977), on a terraced

*Manned space craft take off
from the Kennedy Space Center*

TITUSVILLE

Even those who have never heard of Titusville are likely to know of the **Kennedy Space Center** 2 miles (3km) away. The Center's **Spaceport USA** is fascinating, with plenty to see. **The United States Astronaut Hall of Fame** is located near the entrance to the Space Center. It showcases the country's first astronauts, from their early days through their historic missions during NASA's Mercury program. Sebastian Inlet's **McLarty Museum** shows salvage methods used to recover treasure from the Spanish fleet, which sank in the area in 1715.

WEEKI WACHEE

This famous family attraction is on US19 and Florida 50, 13 miles (21km) west of Brooksville. Centered around a 130-foot-(40m) deep clear natural spring, it's the place to watch underwater shows given by ''mermaids'' (late March to September).

PEACE AND QUIET

Wildlife and Countryside in Florida
by Paul Sterry

Although Florida's summers can be extremely hot and humid, the winters are mild, and this attracts large numbers of visitors from September to May. Florida's wildlife also benefits from the subtropical climate and many of its plants and animals depend upon the mild weather.

Mangrove swamps line the undeveloped stretches of the coast and many of the plants found inland would look equally at home in a South American forest. The birds, too, tend to be more exotic than their counterparts in the rest of the US. Resident species are supplemented during the winter months by migratory birds from Canada and the northern US escaping the ravages of the freezing north. The warm climate also favors cold-blooded animals such as reptiles, amphibians and insects. Most conspicuous of these is the American alligator. Florida juts into the sea, with the Atlantic on the west and the Caribbean on the east. Because of the extensive coastline and favorable climate, much of the coast has been developed into resorts and facilities for tourism. However, despite this, much of interest can still be seen, even among the marinas and other developments.

Tropical plants such as palms flourish in Florida's parks

The Everglades

Florida's southern tip is dominated by the Everglades National Park, a vast wilderness of shallow marsh and grassland covering more than 1½ million acres. Because of the vast distances involved, a car is essential to do justice to the Everglades.

Although interesting throughout the year, the Everglades are perhaps most rewarding during the winter months. This is considered to be the dry season and, as the waters recede, the animals are obliged to congregate around those pools and lakes which remain. Having entered from the park's southern gate, one of the first stops is the Royal Palm Visitor Center. From here you can follow the well-signposted Anhinga Trail. The Anhinga Trail is the park's showpiece and aptly named. Alongside the boardwalk anhingas nest, feed and sunbathe. These primitive-looking birds do not have waterproof feathers, despite their aquatic life-style. Consequently, they have to dry their wings in the sunshine at regular intervals. Alligators on this trail mostly cruise around the water channels but they do occasionally venture up on to the walkways so keep your eyes open!

The reason for the abundance of fish-eating birds and alligators in the Everglades soon becomes apparent when you watch the water; it simply teems with life. The torpedo-shaped garfish is perhaps the most abundant species, but bass and sunfish are also much in evidence. Equally abundant are terrapins and frogs which also feature highly in the diets of the birds and alligators.

From the main entrance to the Everglades, a road runs south for nearly 50 miles (80km), with plenty to see *en route*. Birds of prey are a conspicuous feature of the skies, riding the thermals as soon as the sun warms the ground. Black and turkey vultures are exceedingly common and sometimes feed off carrion beside the road. More elegant is the red-

PEACE AND QUIET

shouldered hawk, which often perches beside the road on low bushes or telephone poles. It is sometimes joined by that most graceful of raptors, the swallowed-tailed kite, which is a summer resident in the Everglades and extremely restricted in its distribution. A variety of mammals can also be seen from the road. Dawn and dusk are the best times to look for white-tailed deer which often graze the grass on the roadside. The charming little marsh rabbit also feeds along the roadside. A night-time drive through the park may reveal the more secretive, nocturnal residents of the Everglades. Several ponds and lakes lie beside FL27. Paurotis Pond and Nine Mile Pond, on the right and left of the road respectively, are good for spotting wildfowl. Mrazek Pond, four miles (6.5km) before Flamingo on the right, and Eco Pond, one mile (1.6km) beyond, are small and allow close views of the birds. Water conditions vary from day to day in each stretch

Alligators are common throughout the Everglades

of water, so it is difficult to predict exactly what will be where. However, you are sure to see snowy egrets with their characteristic yellow "socks," tiny green herons and the inevitable alligator. If you are lucky you may see the aptly-named roseate spoonbill with its strangely flattened bill. Unfortunately, flamingos no longer grace the lakes and shores of Florida, so any large pink bird you see is likely to be a spoonbill.

An alternative point of access to the Everglades is at Shark Valley, on the park's northern boundary. From here you can follow a circular route of 15 miles (24km) along a made-up track through the heart of the Everglades. You can walk the trail, but an interesting mode of transport is to rent a bike and pedal around. The alligators are the most astonishing feature of this trail. Every pool

has its own resident and some of them exceed 10ft (3m) in length. They are most frequently seen sunbathing beside the pool, with their mouths open to help dissipate excess heat. You can sometimes pass within a few feet of these great animals, but it is as well to exercise a degree of caution!

There are a number of larger bodies of water in this part of the Everglades, known as "sloughs." Needless to say, they are a haven for fish and alligators, but they also attract water snakes, which feast on the tadpoles and small fish they contain. Alligators are instrumental in keeping these sloughs open and free from vegetation. Their vigorous wallowing helps prevent plants from colonizing the water

Tricolored herons stalk their prey around watery banks

banks. However, the spikes of the colorful water plant *Pontederia* manage to add a splash of purple to the banks of most pools and sloughs.

On hot days, snakes are often seen crossing the made-up track. Largest and most venomous of these is the Florida cottonmouth, a relative of the rattlesnake but without the rattle. If cornered, these snakes coil up and gape, revealing the soft, white mouths which gave them their name. However, cornering a cottonmouth is absolutely not recommended!

The road which runs along the northern boundary of the park is a good place to watch herons and egrets as they feed in the drainage ditches, but is especially renowned for being the best place to view the scarce everglade or snail kite. The bird flies gracefully over the reeds, occasionally revealing its white rump, while in search of its staple diet, the apple snail. The kite's elongated, curved bill is the perfect tool for "winkling" the snail out of its shell. The road is also a good spot to watch flights of birds at dawn and dusk as they fly to and from their feeding and roosting grounds.

Ponds and Lakes

There are ponds and lakes throughout Florida and they all act as magnets for wildlife. Although they may vary in size from the massive Lake Okeechobee in central Florida to the tiny pools of the Everglades, they are all sure to be worth a visit.

Most ponds and lakes have a shore of reeds and other water plants. These serve as convenient perches for the wealth of water birds which congregate to feed on the fish and amphibians. Largest and most conspicuous of these are the herons and egrets. In addition to the ubiquitous snowy egrets and green herons, patient watching should reveal tricolored and little blue herons and perhaps even a least bittern.

Birdwatching around ponds and lakes in Florida has an advantage over many other areas, in that binoculars are not often needed. Indeed, they can be a positive disadvantage because the birds frequently come too close!

Although many species have lost their fear of humans, they still recognize danger in other forms. Despite their long legs, adapted for wading in deep water, almost all the herons and egrets perch above the water, plunging in only when a meal is in sight. The reason for this apparently peculiar behavior, which is not observed in the same species elsewhere in the US, becomes obvious when you begin to appreciate the number of alligators and snapping turtles that most of the pools hold: to wade in the water is to invite trouble.

American coots are common around the banks of most ponds and lakes. Although superficially similar to their European relatives, a close look reveals a distinctive black mark on the bill and white feathers under the tail. If you are very fortunate, they may be joined by their relative, the American purple gallinule. Generally secretive creatures, gallinules sometimes venture into the open at dawn to bask in the first rays of sun. Ponds and lakes can be found throughout Florida and most have typical wetland wildlife. Try visiting Loxahatchee National Wildlife Refuge inland from Delray Beach. A visitor center and nature trails can be found off US441 between SR804 and SR806. In Fort Lauderdale, visit Royal Palm Park on NW 38th St at NW 17th Avenue, and Rookery Lake Sanctuary on FL27. Lake Ockechobee, on FL27 between Palmdale and Clewiston, is good.

Tropical Forests

Throughout the Everglades and around much of the coast of Florida are found small pockets of tropical forest. Interestingly, they contain species of plants and animals which have closer links with South America than with the temperate forests in neighboring states of the US. Many of these forests, referred to as "hammocks" in the Everglades, are only a few acres in area and are isolated in a sea of grassland, and yet the ages of the trees bear witness to their long-term survival.

Hammocks tend to grow on limestone outcrops and are usually a few feet above the surrounding land. This slight elevation may not seem particularly significant but it provides enough long-term stability to allow trees to grow to a large size. During the wet season, most of the surrounding land is inundated with water, which discourages all but the hardiest of grasses. By contrast, during the dry season, the hammocks retain a lot of moisture in the soil surrounding the roots. As a consequence they are less prone to damage from the dry season fires which can sweep through the surrounding grassland.

Many of the tropical hammocks in the Everglades have superb boardwalks, giving visitors access to the forest while at the same time preventing damage to the vegetation. Entering a hammock is like walking into a different world. Gone is the intense heat of the sun, replaced with dappled sunlight and cool, humid air. Strangler figs grapple their way up their hosts' trunks towards the tree canopy, eventually to constrict their benefactors to death.

At ground level, prickly pear cacti grow in clearings, while above them the branches and trunks of the trees are festooned with epiphytic plants – plants without roots in soil which grow instead on other plants. In most cases the epiphytes cause no direct harm to the plant they live on apart from adding to its weight. Most striking of these plants are the bromeliads, or "air-plants," with spiky rosettes

of leaves and colorful flowers.
Good examples of hammocks
of tropical forest can be found
along the Gumbo Limbo trail at
Royal Palm Hammock, just
beyond the visitor center for
the Everglades National Park.
Also visit Mahogany Hammock,
one mile (1.6km) west of FL27,
approximately 20 miles (32km)
beyond the visitor center.

The Keys

The Keys conjure up romantic
images of the Caribbean, with
exotic beaches and
aquamarine seas. The reality is
different. Development has
encroached on all but a few
pockets of natural vegetation.
However, it is not all bad news;
almost every golf course has a
thriving population of
burrowing owls and white
ibises adorning the greens.
The Keys are a chain of islands
which stretch south from the tip
of Florida for nearly 90 miles
(145km). Nowadays, a road
(US1) links them all so that it is
possible to drive from Miami
to Key West in a day. Along
most of the route there are
power lines and telegraph
poles, which serve as perches
for the exotic scissor-tailed
flycatcher, a regular winter
visitor.
Waders and terns are common
and a careful eye on the skies
should eventually reveal a truly
exotic speciality of the Keys, the
magnificent frigatebird. With a
wingspan of over 8ft (2.5m)
these birds soar effortlessly on
the sea breeze, harassing other
seabirds into regurgitating their
last meal, which the frigatebirds
then catch and eat! However,

the most spectacular bird of the
Keys must surely be the great
white heron, an immense bird
which stands nearly 5ft (1.5m)
tall. It is found only in the Keys.
There are still a few remnants of
natural vegetation to be seen,
such as mangrove swamps and
slash pine forests. The best
examples are to be found on
Big Pine Key, where there are
several wildlife refuges and the
undergrowth includes an
endemic species of prickly
pear, Spanish moss and exotic-
looking yuccas. Big Pine Key is,
perhaps, best known for the
charming key deer. This dog-
sized animal has its only
stronghold on this Key. Small
groups often venture out of the
undergrowth at dusk to browse
beside the road and provide
wonderful views. Visitors
should be particularly careful
when driving on Big Pine Key
because unfortunately dozens
of the delightful creatures are
accidentally killed each year by
cars.

A stately great white heron

Cypress Swamps

Many of Florida's wet woodland areas have been drained, but a few still survive under the protection of a variety of conservation organizations. The wettest woodlands are known as cypress swamps. Perhaps the best example is the National Audubon Society's Corkscrew Swamp, near the small town of Immokalee.

The drier parts of the wood are composed of slash pine, but as the water level rises this gives way to cypresses. The trees are festooned with exotic epiphytic orchids, ferns and lichens, with great creepers reaching for the skies. Fortunate visitors may see the elusive river otter but the Florida race of the fox squirrel is more conspicuous, distinguished by its black face. Birds, too, are abundant in Corkscrew Swamp. The large and noisy pileated woodpecker drills dead timber in search of grubs. Herons and egrets stalk fish in the open channels of water. Little blue herons are often seen trotting across the carpets of water lettuce. There are a few pairs of wood storks nesting in trees. At dawn and dusk the feeding birds are sometimes joined by a limpkin, a secretive ibis-like bird whose extraordinary nocturnal calls are unforgettable.

As the cypress trees age they die and fall, leaving stumps which gradually become eroded into pinnacles of wood. These provide ideal perches for the barred owl, one of the most spectacular birds to be seen in this habitat.

Pine Forests

Pine forests are widespread throughout the state of Florida. Three of the largest forests are the Apalachicola National Forest (557,000 acres) in the Panhandle, the Ocala National Forest (366,000 acres) and the Osceola National Forest (157,000 acres) near Lake City. Seven species of native pine occur in Florida, but the slash pine predominates throughout most of the state. A carpet of fallen pine needles and cabbage palms prevents an extensive ground flora from developing, but spikes of lady's tresses orchids can be seen. Common anole lizards and skinks scuttle among the ground vegetation and several species of snake are found in most woodlands.

Woodlands contain many species of mammal. The well-named armadillo roots in the soil for food and can occasionally be located by this sound, but the bobcat is much quieter and a good deal of luck will be needed to see one.

Listen for rustling in the ground vegetation and you may see a party of boldly marked bobwhite quails.

Shell Collecting

A description of Florida would not be complete without mentioning the shells for which the state is famous. Almost every beach has a good selection of species but some, such as Sanibel, Cape Sable and Marathon Key are

renowned and the remarkable subtropical shells such as conches, murex and couries immediately catch the eye. Regrettably, many avid shell collectors are only interested in the shells of living animals. Many species are under threat, so that in certain areas collectors are restricted to two live animals of each species. It is also worth remembering that shells for sale in the shops will almost certainly have been stolen from living creatures and so are best avoided.

Screw pine on the Florida Keys (below) and (above) a barred owl

FOOD AND DRINK

Think of orange juice and you've thought of Florida, for the state claims to produce 25 percent of the world's orange crop and 95 percent of all orange juice concentrate. Fresh fruit is readily available. Orlando was an early citrus center – and indeed, there are still groves upon groves in the area. Exotic fruits have joined the more common variety, and interesting jams, marmalades and chutneys are for sale in the gourmet food markets.

In recent years, the state has been experimenting with fruit wines, but there are perhaps not enough accolades to warrant recommendation. Do

About a third of Florida's agricultural yield comes from oranges, grapefruit and tangerines

however, try the local (albeit rare) white tupelo honey if possible.

Some time ago, the cattle industry was big business in Florida, an important preface to agriculture, and beef is still a menu staple these days. You will find some of the state's most succulent steaks in Tampa, at Bern's – a huge steak house with a wine list to match. But it is with seafood that this state comes into its own.

Florida's waters have always provided a steady food supply. Even the earliest settlers did no lack for shellfish; but it was the development of quick-freezing processes which made seafood and freshwater fish production a commercial industry.

You can hardly go wrong dining out at one of Florida's countless fish restaurants, where there is usually a choice of clams, shrimp, oysters, snapper, crawfish or local lobster. Scamp, by the way, is not a misspelling of scampi, but a fish in its own right – white and flaky and related to the grouper family. It is scarce, but try it if you have the chance. Stone crabs are another delicacy, in season in winter and a speciality at several Miami establishments.

Ethnic Food

Florida's food is as diverse as the people who live here. There are only remnants of Native American cuisine, such as cassava pie and corn fritters, but the Cubans, who have considerably swelled the population, have brought their taste for spicy fare with them. That means black beans with everything and sweet black coffee afterwards. The influence is at its strongest on Calle Ocho in downtown Miami and in Ybor City, the Latin section of Tampa and home to Florida's oldest restaurant – The Columbia – first opened in 1905 and naturally offering Spanish cuisine. There is also a sizeable Greek community centered around Tarpon Springs, where so many tavernas are serving up

moussaka and keftedes it seems like a miniature Athens! Down in the Keys, look on menus for conch fritters and Key Lime pie. The conch (pronounced "conk") is a delicious edible mollusk. It is also the colloquial name given to island-born Key Westers, who are descendants of a Cuban, Yankee seafarer and British loyalist mix. Key Lime pie, a pastry shell filled with a mixture of condensed milk, lime juice, eggs and sugar, topped with meringue, baked and served cold – now popular throughout the States – should, if it's authentic, be colored cream, not green.

In St Augustine, you may notice a Minorcan influence on some of the restaurant menus here – highly seasoned stews made with chicken, pork and seafood mixed with rice, beans and peppers. You can also find cheese turnovers and *picadillo*, seasoned ground beef mixed with olives, raisins and onions.

Places to Eat

Florida offers a variety of cuisine at acceptable prices. Seafood restaurants are an adventure in themselves and represent good value at between $6 and $12 per person. There is also a choice of steak houses, bufffet-style cafeterias, and authentic southern style diners where supper is often only $4 to $6 a head. You will of couse pay for the pleasure of dining at more upscale restaurants, but even then look for chalkboard specials!

SHOPPING

Visitors won't lack for places in which to buy or browse. Wherever there's a spare niche, there's a boutique or souvenir stand; wherever there's space, a new mall or center goes up. Renewed preservation efforts continue into the 1990s and more and more historic districts are being restored. Gift shops and art galleries usually spring up simultaneously. And many areas where merchandise is for sale are designed with a theme (a fishing village, perhaps), or reflect an ethnic character (Greek in Tarpon Springs, Spanish in Ybor City) or a particular era. Some of the shopping streets and strips are particularly famous, like Coral Gables' "Miracle Mile" where all the leading brand names in clothing are sold.

Your budget may not stretch to the prices in the windows along Las Olas Boulevard in Fort Lauderdale or Worth Avenue in Palm Beach, but who can resist a saunter down either?

A long established but still chic Miami area is Bal Harbour with notable department stores such as Saks and Neiman-Marcus. Coconut Grove, south of Miami, is Florida's

A replica of HMS Bounty, *scene of the infamous 1789 mutiny, lies in Biscayne Bay*

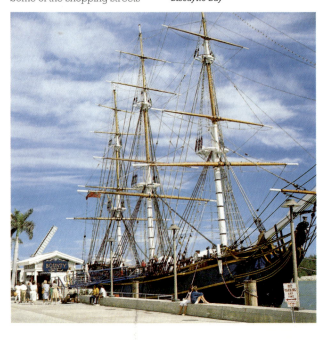

Greenwich Village, with hundreds of chic upscale shops and restaurants. One of the best ethnic areas is Calle Ocho in downtown Miami (South West 8th Street) which has been developed as Miami's Latin Quarter. Here you'll find bakeries selling sweet Cuban pastries, and small cigar factories where the product is still hand rolled. Ybor City is Tampa's picturesque Latin Quarter, and here, too, new life has been injected. Ybor Square's shops, for example, now brim with antiques, arts and plants, and many new additions are expected. "Nostalgia Market" offers bygones from open stalls.

A new Miami pride is the newly completed downtown Bayside Marketplace, a $93 million waterfront speciality shop center where you'll find upscale boutiques as well as international food stands and restaurants. Downtown Orlando's popular Church Street Station has undergone a $60 million expansion, which included the opening of the Church Street Exchange, a festive three-level shopping area with speciality shops and restaurants in Victorian style. To find discount centers and factory outlets, where you can pick up brand named goods for a lesser price than in the upscale stores, it is best to look at local tourist publications and newspapers when you arrive in Florida, whatever your base. But to give you some idea, the Quality Outlet Center on International Drive in Orlando features brand name factory outlets which include Corning (a good spot to look for kitchenware), Fostoria Glass, top-labeled men's clothing, Great Western Boots and women's fashions.

Since Orlando and its vicinity are likely to take top priority on your vacation itinerary, you may well want to visit The Florida Mall at the Intersection of 441 and 482 for its 150 stores; La Mirada, over 90 speciality shops midway between the Florida Turnpike and Interstate 4; Mangate Mall in Kissimmee (close to the Magic Kingdom entrance) with more than 80 stores; and Osceola Square Mall, 84 stores on West Highway 192 in Kissimmee. Old Town, designed in turn-of-the-century style, is a well-established tourist attraction featuring over 100 stores. Theme parks also provide an infinite variety of shops. At Disney World, for example, all the resort hotels have their own shops; as do Magic Kingdom's Main Street and EPCOT's World Showcase pavilions. Then there's Walt Disney World Shopping Village, where boutiques sell a variety of merchandise, from Christmas decorations to children's wear and nautical gifts. Disney soft toys are, of course, in abundant supply. And Mickey Mouse hats are available everywhere. There are shopping bazaars in the Morocco and Stanleyville sections of the Busch Gardens theme park near Tampa.

What you buy naturally depends very much on you. Resort wear is always a good buy – and a natural buy in Florida, with its year-round resort weather. Every imaginable oddity also seems to be available.

Tarpon Springs' infinite variety of sponges, from back scratchers to car washers, are a good value at the price. Miami's Latin Quarter and Tampa's Ybor City have ample supplies of good cigars. You could buy your shells in the Caribbean but they're much cheaper in the Gulf islands off Florida.

ACCOMMODATIONS

Florida accommodations run the gamut from budget motels to plush resorts as well as a growing number of all-suite properties. Motels offer particularly good value for families (the better ones have restaurant and recreational facilities) since one price pays for a room that can often sleep four people.

They are located along the state highways and beaches and close to popular visitor areas like Disney World and the Everglades. A number of them are members of a chain such as Hilton, Howard Johnson or Day's Inn, all of a high-lodging standard.

Short-term rental apartments and villas are an alternative way of keeping costs down and the choice is enormous. Here again, general standards are high – apartments are often situated in complexes with their own swimming pools and golf courses, etc. Bed and breakfast in private homes is also available, through bed and breakfast associations.

Bear in mind that a b&b is not necessarily cheaper than a motel, but your accommodation *can* be much more charming. There are also plenty of glamorous resort hotels in Florida, especially on the east coast, if cost is not of prime importance. Such hotels usually have every conceivable facility on site – from tennis courts to golf courses, and more. If cost is a consideration, go in the low season – generally from May through September for south Florida, and November through March for the north of the state – with rates for hotels or motels from $30 per night (based on double occupancy). Or rent a room a block or more from the beach, where you will save dollars but still be only a short walk from the shore.

NIGHTLIFE

There is no shortage of cultural and light entertainment in the cities, where there are numerous performing arts centers, theaters and nightclubs. Top name entertainers frequently appear in Miami at the large hotels, and clubs here often feature lavish revues. Nightlife is also lively in the Orlando area, including Disney World itself. Details of current shows are available in local papers and visitor publications.

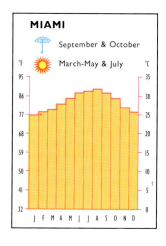

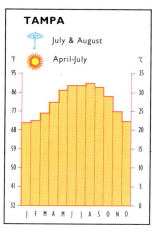

WEATHER AND WHEN TO GO

Although summer temperatures are pretty uniform in all parts of Florida – probably in the 80s Fahrenheit (30s C), winter climates can vary. Average January temperatures, for example, range from around 52 degrees Fahrenheit (10 degrees Centigrade) in the northwest to 67 degrees Fahrenheit (18 degrees Centigrade) along the lower coast and 70 degrees Fahrenheit (21 degrees Centigrade) in the Keys. In the brief cool winter coastal regions will be warmer than inland, due to the influence of the Gulf and Atlantic. Rainfall is heaviest from July to October. The top luxury resort hotels will expect some formality of dress in the evening although the jacket and tie rule is not used generally. Normally, summer resort wear that is cool, casual and comfortable, is more than adequate. Add a shawl, jacket or sweater for the odd cool winter spell or as a precaution against icy air-conditioning.

CHILDREN

If there is one state which specifically appeals to children, that state is Florida. There are so many theme parks and family orientated attractions that the choice is almost overwhelming. The Orlando area alone is surely unrivaled. Disney World quite apart, there is a host of other theme parks, animal and bird shows, wax museums, alligator centers, amusement arcades, thrill rides, zoos and marine parks. But be selective; entrance fees can mount up. In the case of the best known attractions (Disney World, MGM Studios Theme Park, Universal Studios, Cypress Gardens, Busch Gardens etc) charges are quite high, but they do cover all the rides and attractions. In some cases passes are included in vacation packages.

Florida's beach choice is huge, too. The offshore islands to the west are unspoiled and quiet and will not be suited to active kids who like fairgrounds and video arcades; nor is there much to do in most of the Keys apart from watersports. Both the Pinellas and the Gold Coast resorts, however, have enough to please all ages.

Museums in Florida often encourage visitor participation with hands-on exhibits to keep everyone amused. Well-endowed science museums always feature such galleries, and often boast a planetarium as well. History is brought alive by the use of craft and other demonstrations, and costumed guides. Other cultural heritage is handled similarly – at Florida's Native American villages for example.

All in all, the Sunshine State can generally keep children happy, if not ecstatic, for weeks on end.

A touch of tropical color from a macaw in Cypress Gardens near Winter Haven

FESTIVALS AND EVENTS

Innumerable festivals and events take place all over Florida. Local newspapers and visitor publications will tell you what's going on. Among the highlights are:

JANUARY
Jacksonville – Gator Bowl Football Classic
Daytona Beach – 24-hr race
Homestead – Annual rodeo
Miami Beach – Art Deco Weekend
Fort Lauderdale – Flagler Day
Coral Gables – Miracle Mile Art Show
West Palm Beach – Polo & Country Club season, Silver Sailfish Derby
Orlando – Highland Games
Sarasota – Annual Shell Show
Tarpon Springs – Epiphany Day
Key West – Art Explo Craft Show

FEBRUARY
Palatka – Azalea Festival
Olustee – Battle of Olustee

St Augustine – Menendez Day
Daytona Beach – Daytona 500
Coconut Grove – Arts Festival
Miami Beach – Arts Festival
Miami – Grand Prix and International Festival, Boat Show
Key West – Old Island Days
Orlando – Central Florida Fair
Winter Haven – Florida Citrus Festival
Cape Coral – Annual Outdoor Arts & Crafts Show
Sarasota – Asolo State Theater Season
Fort Myers Beach – Estero Island Shrimp Festival
Plant City – Florida Strawberry Festival
Tampa – Gasparilla Pirate Invasion, Ybor City Fiesta Day

MARCH

Miami – Renaissance Fair
Daytona Beach – Cycle Week
Miami – Calle Ocho Open House, Carnaval Miami
Fort Lauderdale – Las Olas Art Festival
Lignumvitae Key – Lignumvitae Blossom Festival
West Palm Beach – Arts Festival
Orlando – Central Florida Fair
Arcadia – All-Florida Championship Rodeo
Dunedin – Highland Games
Tampa – Latin American Fiesta
Sanibel Island – Shell Fair
Kissimmee – Blue Grass Festival
Sarasota – Medieval Fair
Fort Myers – Shrimp Festival

APRIL

St Augustine – Arts & Crafts Festival, Blessing of the Fleet
Palatka – District Rodeo
Jacksonville and Dunedin – Highland Games

Gainesville – Arts Festival
Daytona Beach – Music Festival
Cocoa Beach – Pro-Am Surfing Festival

MAY

Miami – Seafood Festival, Miami River Regatta
Sarasota – International Sandcastle Contest
Pensacola – Festival of Five Flags

JUNE

Daytona Beach – Summer Speed Week
Delray Beach – State tennis championships
Coconut Grove – Goombay Festival
Miami Beach – Indoor Flea Market

JULY

Jacksonville – Shell Show
Daytona Beach – Firecracker 400, Paul Devere 250
Miami – Outdoor Music Festival
Key West – Hemingway Days
Kissimmee – Silver Spurs Rodeo
Arcadia – All-Florida Rodeo

AUGUST

Boca Raton – Boca Festival
Fort Walton Beach – Billfish Tournament

SEPTEMBER

Cocoa Beach – Florida Pro International Surfing Contest
Key West – Oyster Season
Miami and Orlando – Oktoberfests

OCTOBER

Miami – Hispanic Heritage Festival

NOVEMBER
St Augustine – Fall Arts &
Crafts Festival
Miami – Greek Festival, Arts
Festival
Orlando – Pioneer Days
Apalachicola – Florida
Seafood Festival

HOW TO BE A LOCAL

If you happen to have blue
rinsed hair and don't mind
whether or not you look good
in a colorful shirt or skirt, you
will certainly fit into the Miami
or St Petersburg picture very
well.

Many so-called Floridians,
known around here as
"Snowbirds," have actually
retired here from colder
climes.

But the really local populace
is both young and fun loving,
favoring the outdoor life and
tootling about on boats. This
is no more so than in the Keys
where the pace is particularly
laid back. The Floridian is
sporty, but just as likely only
to dabble in fishing as to take
it seriously.

Whatever your age, if you're
young at heart, you'll be
delighted by Florida and
Florida will be delighted by
you. It may have been
outsiders who saw the
potential and developed the
plethora of theme parks, but
the residents have a relaxed
joy about them too. Though
many of the attractions are
human-made, there are still
natural ones that haven't been
destroyed where wildlife is
left in peace in the giant tracts
of swamp and forest that
cover chunks of the state.

If you love the feeling of sand
between your toes, the taste of
succulent seafood, can let your
hair down on a whim, you're
well on the way to becoming
Floridianized – it's a state of
mind.

TIGHT BUDGET TIPS

- Stay at a motel – many
  provide two double beds, so
  that children can stay with
  parents for the same price
  (age limits can vary from
  12–18).

- Opt for eating in – Florida
  has a huge number of
  exceptionally well-equipped
  units with kitchens, many of
  which can be booked
  through travel agents.

- East fast food – it may not be
  elegant, but it is economical.
  Look out for children's
  menus and fixed-price all-
  you-can-eat signs. Diners
  offer excellent value for
  breakfast.

- If you want to rent a car, do
  some homework – many
  tour operators offer very
  good fly/drive deals.
  Otherwise you may find
  that small local firms offer
  cheaper rental rates than
  some of the big international
  companies.

- Check the local papers and
  visitors' guides for
  admission-free places
  before you plan your day.

- Entrance fees in theme
  parks can mount up. Make
  a top-priority list and stick
  to it.

- Buy stamps at a post office,
  not from a machine.

DIRECTORY

Arriving

Florida boasts three international airports. Miami is the major air terminal for Florida, with direct flights from many US cities. Tampa, serving Florida's Gulf Coast area, has an almost equal number of flight connections. Orlando, serving Florida's interior resort areas, including Disney World, has been the fastest growing airport and is considered the most modern and best planned. It is served by some 24 carriers with direct services from over 100 cities worldwide. Most domestic airlines, including Delta, TWA, USAir and Continental, schedule regular flights into Florida. Air connection between Florida cities are frequent. Flights between points such as Miami and the Keys are reasonably priced, but planes are small and bookings can be heavy.
Airport Transfers Many hotels and resorts in Florida provide complimentary transportation, usually by airport limousine, between airport and hotel. Otherwise:
Miami Has a 24-hour bus service from the airport to the downtown bus terminal (travel time 25 minutes), and hotels on request. By public transportation – bus number 20 leaves every half hour from 6:00A.M. to 1:00A.M., while Greyhound runs services to Homestead, Islamorada, Key Largo, Key West and Marathon. Taxis and limousines are also available.
Tampa Buses run to downtown Tampa – travel time 15 minutes. Limousines and taxis also available.
Orlando A number of bus shuttle and limousine services take you to downtown Orlando, International Drive, or Lake Buena Vista – fares from $10 to $25 (children, $5 to $15).

Camping

Florida has more campgrounds and campsites than any other state. They are to be found in almost every national or state park, forest and recreational area, including Disney World. Most are open all year and have electrical hook-ups, a supplies store and leisure facilities. The *Florida Camping Directory*, published annually, gives full details of some of the best campgrounds/sites; it is available free, from Florida Campground Association, Department D–8, 1638 N. Plaza Drive, Tallahassee, FL 32308-5323 (tel: (904) 656 8878).

Car Breakdown
See **Emergency Road Services**

Car Rental
See **Domestic Travel** (sub-heading, **Driving**)

Chauffeur Driven Cars

Easy to arrange but not cheap. Many hotels and motels in the tourist areas provide a complimentary limousine service to and from airports. A "public" limousine service performs a shuttle service between airport and hotel for less than the cost of a taxi, but should not be confused with

Florida has plenty of car rental choice – and the lowest US prices

the more luxurious, sedan-type, private limousine. Bookings for chauffeur drive may be made in advance through one of the car rental companies.

Contacts

Hotels and Motels: Florida Hotel/Motel Association, P.O. Box 1529, Tallahassee, Fl 32302 (tel: (904) 224 2888).

Attractions: Florida Atttractions Association, P.O. Box 10925, Tallahassee, FL 32302 (tel: (904) 222 2885).

Historical Sites: Department of State, Bureau of Historic Preservation, R.A. Gray Building, 500 S Bronough St, Tallahassee, FL 32399-0250 (tel: (904) 487 2333).

National Forests: U.S. Forest Service, Suite 4061, 227 N Bronough St, Tallahassee, FL 32301 (tel: (904) 681 7265).

State Forests: Department of Agriculture and Consumer Services, Division of Forestry, 3125 Conner Blvd, Tallahassee, FL 32399-1650 (tel: (904) 488 6727).

State Parks: Department of Natural Resources, Office of Communications, 3900 Commonwealth Blvd, Tallahassee, FL 32399-3000 (tel: (904) 488 7326).

Crime

Like most major cities, neither Miami nor Tampa is crime-free. However, if common sense prevails (ie: don't walk down dark alleys at night, don't carry large sums of money), tourists' safety is as reasonable as anywhere. Throughout Florida, beware of thieves who will try to grab your purse through a car window or unlocked door while your car is stopped at a light. Keep all car doors locked for safety.

Domestic Travel
Air (see **Arriving**)

Driving You need a valid driver's licence to rent a car in Florida, of course. Usually you must be 21 more. Gas remains more reasonable than in many other destinations. The speed limit in Florida is 55 miles (88km) per hour. In cities and congested areas though it is generally between 20-40 miles (32-64km) per hour and 15 miles (24km) per hour in school zones. Road signs indicate specific limits and those are strictly enforced. Alamo Rent-a-Car is one of the most popular car rental firms in Florida, and a partner in many of the fly drive packages, but other companies such as Avis, Budget, Hertz, Dollar and Thrifty also have a major presence. Each offers its own packages and discounts, but in any case car rental is cheaper in this state than in any other. It should be noted that some car rental companies will **not** accept cash – you will need one of the major credit cards. Also there may be a surcharge for drivers under 25. Some operators feature fly/drive programs here, often including free use of a car for a specific period. However, do ensure that the size of vehicle being offered is suitable to the size of your family and the length of journey planned – a family of four will not be comfortable on a long trip in a compact and luggage space may be insufficient; it might be better to pay extra for a larger model. If a driving tour is planned, make sure that unlimited mileage is included (for instance, cars rented in Florida from Alamo may *only* be driven in Florida and Georgia; USA Rent-a-Car restricts you to Florida only). Collision damage waiver (CDW), though, usually has to be arranged independently – and is strongly recommended; otherwise in the event of an accident you will be liable for the cost of repairs up to the full value of the car. Some credit cards include this coverage if you use them to pay for the rental

car; check with your credit card provider for details. Finally, Florida possesses inaptly named "lovebugs" – extremely sticky and acidic insects that swarm during daylight hours in spring and autumn, clogging radiators and windshields. During these times restrict driving to early morning or late afternoon and drive at lower speeds.

Car Rental Companies Alamo Rent-A-Car, P.O. Box 22776, Fort Lauderdale, FL 33335 (tel: (305) 522 0000). Avis Rent-A-Car, 2330 NW 37th Ave, Miami, FL 33142 (tel: (305) 635 7777). Budget Rent-A-Car, P.O. Box 540509, Orlando, FL 32801 (tel: (407) 423 4141). Dollar Rent-A-Car, 5012 W Lemon St, Tampa, FL 33609 (tel: (813) 276 3772). Hertz Rent-A-Car, 520 N Semoran Blvd, Orlando, FL 32807 (tel: (407) 275 6430). National Car Rental, 2301 NW 33rd Ave, Miami, FL 33142 (tel: (305) 638 5900). Payless Car Rental, 5510 Gulfport Blvd, St Petersburgh, FL 33707 (tel: (813) 381 2758). Thrifty Car Rental, 2701 NW Lejeune Rd, Miami, FL 33142 (tel: (305) 871 2277).

Bus Greyhound Lines operates an inter-city service between 85 Florida cities. Greyhound does not have a toll free number, but your local terminal should be able to provide information on fares, destinations, and more. Local communities, including the major cities of Miami, Orlando and Tampa are served by local buses. Miami, in addition, is served by an elevated metrorail service into the downtown area connecting to an automated People Mover rail line, and Tampa by its People Mover rail line connecting the business district with Harbour Island.

Taxi These are plentiful and, except for airport zone trips, operate on a metered system. If vacant (with the light on), they may be hailed on the street; phoned for; or found at stands in city centers and outside major hotels. Taxis charge a fixed flat rate, plus an additional fee based on distance. In Miami they can be expensive.

Rail Inter-city rail service, with Miami stations southernmost point, is provided by Amtrak.

Emergency Road Service

The American Automobile Association, AAA, operates a nationwide emergency road service number to assist members in case of difficulties with their cars. If you require emergency assistance call 1-800-222-7764 and you will be given information. If you are involved in a traffic accident it must be reported at once to the local police station, County Sheriff's Office, or Florida Highway Patrol.

Emergency Telephone Numbers

There is no nationwide emergency system in Florida. There are emergency numbers you can call, and these are sometimes indicated on pay phones, but they vary from place to place. In any emergency, it is best for an

out-of-state visitor to call the police, who will put you in contact with the appropriate service if they cannot help – dial 911 (free call) in the Miami, Orlando and Tampa areas. Otherwise the best thing to do is call the operator by dialing '0' and ask to be connected to the service you require.

Handicapped Visitors

Most buildings in Florida are required by law to provide access to handicapped persons. Contact the Florida Division of Tourism (see **Tourist Offices** for address) for further details.

Health

It cannot be emphasized enough that arranging medical insurance before traveling is essential. Insurance coverage for an unlimited amount of medical costs is recommended. Treatment (unless an emergency) will be refused without evidence of insurance or a deposit. If you need a doctor during your stay, ask at your hotel or look in the Yellow Pages under "Physician." See also **Pharmacist**, below. No inoculations are required for a visit to Florida, but it is a rabies risk area. Tap water is generally considered safe to drink.

Holidays – Public

New Year's Day (Jan 1), Martin Luther King Jr's Birthday (third Monday in Jan), Washington's Birthday (third Mon in Feb), Good Friday, Memorial Day (last Mon in May),

Independence Day (July 4), Labor Day (first Mon in Sept), Columbus Day (second Mon in Oct), Veterans' Day (Nov 11), Thanksgiving Day (fourth Thurs in Nov), Christmas Day.

Money Matters

Overseas visitors note: as a general rule, banks are open from 9:00A.M. to 3:00P.M. Monday–Friday and are closed on weekends and public holidays, although in some major towns and tourist areas hours may be longer. It is best to take travelers' checks. The advantage of this is that travelers' checks can be used very much like cash and in most cases offer protection against theft. Hotels, restaurants, gas stations and stores in Florida will accept them as cash and give change where necessary. It is a useful way of topping up your cash supply without going to the bank (in any case, many banks do not have the facility to cash travelers' checks, and those that do are likely to charge a high commission). For this reason it is advisable to take out travelers' checks in denominations of $10 or $20. Remember that Florida levies a 6 percent sales tax on goods (except "necessary" food purchased in grocery stores), so the price tag you see may not be the price you pay. An additional Resort Tax applies to hotels and restaurants, and sometimes a convention tax is levied on hotels. Rates vary between municipalities, but the final bill could have up to 11 percent added in tax.

You can use credit cards almost anywhere. All the major cards are accepted throughout Florida.

Opening Times

Shopping Malls: 10:00A.M. 9:00P.M. Monday–Saturday, some open 7 days a week closing at 6:00P.M on Sundays. **Downtown shops:** 10:00A.M. to 6:00P.M. Monday– Saturday. **Banks:** (see **Money Matters**).

Pharmacists

Over-the-counter medicines are readily available at any pharmacy (drugstore).

Places of Worship

Churches of all denominations will be found in the major cities. Check times of services and locations in local newspapers or with hotels.

Post Offices

Post office hours do vary both in central city branches and in small towns, so it is best to check at the hotel. Stamps, however, may be purchased in hotels, motels, drugstores and transportation terminals, usually by inserting correct change into a machine, though these charge 25 percent more. (You will have no trouble finding souvenir postcards.)

Publications

Miami/South Florida is a monthly magazine, available from newsstands – it contains an events section for the area for that month.

See Orlando is a free monthly magazine providing information on the city's attractions, shopping areas, restaurants and nightclubs. Copies are distributed at hotels and motels throughout the city.

Senior Citizens

Florida probably attracts more elderly people than any other state, and although senior citizen discounts are common throughout the state, they are not clearly displayed. Your best bet simply is to ask whether there is a senior citizen discount available on any purchase, meal, hotel stay or attraction.

Sport and Recreation

Florida is a sports-oriented state, for both participants and spectators and pastimes are diverse enough to suit any taste. Among the most popular spectator sports for the latter are the motor races in Daytona Beach, horse racing at Hialeah, jai-alai in Miami, and football. The rodeos at Kissimmee, Homestead and Arcadia are state events. There are plenty of dog racing tracks throughout the state. For participatory sports, Florida specializes in the water variety. With miles of inland and coastal waterways and innumerable marinas, boating of all kinds is a way of life, from canoeing to cruising. The Florida Canoe Trail System encompasses 35 rivers and waterways. There are unlimited possibilities for fishing and underwater exploration. Many resort properties offer a full range of watersports and equipment rental, which often includes instruction, as well as facilities for other sports, such as horse back riding, tennis and golf. Hiking is also a very

popular pastime, particularly along the 1,000 miles (1,600km) of the Florida Trail. To find out more about certain sports and activities there are contact addresses:

Boating (Registration and regulations) – Department of Natural Resources, Office of Communications, 3900 Commonwealth Blvd, Tallahassee, FL 32399-3000 (tel: (904) 488 1195).

Diving – Department of Commerce, Division of Tourism, Office of Sports Promotion, Collins Building, Suite 510E, Tallahassee, FL 32399-2000 (tel: (904) 488 8347).

Fishing and Hunting – Game and Freshwater Fish Commission, 620 S Meridan St, Farris Bryant Building, Tallahassee, FL 32399-1600 (tel: (904) 488 1960).

Golf – Florida State Golf Association, P.O. Box 21177, Sarasota, FL 34238 (tel: (813) 921 5695).

Tennis – Florida Tennis Association, 801 NE 167 St, Suite 301, North Miami Beach, FL 33162 (tel: (305) 652 2866).

Student and Youth Travel

Some operators specialize in travel for young people and/or exchange programs. Florida boasts many youth hostels, including those near Ocala National Forest and Disney World. Some attractions offer a special admission price for students and there are student concessions for some regular rail fares.

Telephones

Florida is divided into four telephone regions, with the area codes of 305, 813, 407 and 904. To call long distance within the area code, dial 1 plus telephone number. To call outside the area code, dial 1, plus area code, plus telephone number. For direct dialing of international calls dial 011, plus country code, plus city code (omit the initial 0 or 9; 15 or 16 for France), plus telephone number. If you use your hotel room phone, expect to pay a premium.

Time, Local

Most of Florida is on Eastern Standard Time. Part of the northwest, including Pensacola and Fort Walton Beach is on Central Time, an hour behind the rest of Florida.

Tipping

Tipping is common practice. The majority of hotels in Florida do not include a service charge in their bills. As a general rule visitors should tip porters 50 cents per bag; taxi drivers, 15 percent of fare; hotel chambermaids, $2 per night; and in restaurants or hairdressers, 10-20 percent of the bill.

Sea and sunshine make Florida the ideal state for water sports

Toilets

Public toilets throughout
Florida and particularly in the
popular theme parks like
Disney World and EPCOT are
almost always of a high
standard.

Tour Operators

Tour operators can arrange
packages to meet the specific
needs of the visitor. Such
agencies include:
Go Florida!, 1666 Kennedy
Causeway, North Bay Village,
FL 33141 (tel: (305) 866 5555);
Florida Destinations,
1200 Anastasia Ave, Coral
Gables, FL 33134
(tel: (305) 443 7706);
Ving Florida, 18555 Collins
Ave, Miami Beach, FL 33160
(tel: (305) 935 3904).

Tourist Offices

For information in the US on
the whole of the state of
Florida contact:
Office of Visitor Inquiry,
Florida Division of Tourism,
126 West Van Buren Street,
Tallahassee, Fl 32399-2000.
(tel: (904) 487 1462).
The Florida Division of
Tourism has a London office
(tel: (071) 727 1661). In
Germany, the address is
Schillerstrasse 10, Frankfurt.
The Florida Division of
Tourism operates visitor
centers in major towns and
resorts including:

Northwest

200 W College Ave,
Tallahassee, FL 32302
(tel: (904) 681 9200).
1401 E Gregory St, **Pensacola**,
FL 32501 (tel: (904) 434 1234).

Northeast

6 East Bay St, Suite 200,
Jacksonville, FL 32202
(tel: (904) 353 9736).

Central

1925 E Irlo Bronson Memorial
Highway, **Kissimmee**,
FL 34744 (tel: (407) 847 5000).
(For Kissimmee/St Cloud.) 7208
Sand Lake Rd, Suite 300,
Orlando, FL 32819
(tel: (407) 363 5800). (For
Orlando and Orange County.)

Central West

4625 East Bay Dr, Suite 109,
Clearwater, FL 34624
(tel: (813) 530 6452). (For
Pinellas County.)
111 Madison St, Suite 1010,
Tampa, FL 33602
(tel: (813) 223 1111).

Southwest

2180 W First St, **Fort Myers**,
FL 33901 (tel: (813) 335 2631).
(For Lee County.)

Southeast

500 E Broward Blvd, **Fort
Lauderdale**, FL 33394
(tel: (305) 765 4466).
701 Brickell Ave, Suite 2700,
Miami, FL 33131
(tel: (305) 539 3000).
1555 Palm Beach Lakes Blvd,
West Palm Beach, FL 33401
(tel: (407) 471 3995). (For Palm
Beach County.)
There are also visitor centers
at roadside locations on US 231
at Campbellton, US 301 at
Hilliard, I-75 near Jennings, I-10
at Pensacola, and on I-95 near
Yulee. For more specific
information, ask for the local
chambers of commerce in the
area you wish to visit.

INDEX